Bill O'Reilly
Versus
The Truth

Bill O'Reilly
Versus
The Truth

◆

Confronting The Propaganda Of Bill O'Reilly And The Scam Of The "No-Spin" Zone

Roy Chowthi

iUniverse, Inc.

New York Lincoln Shanghai

Bill O'Reilly Versus The Truth
Confronting The Propaganda Of Bill O'Reilly And The Scam Of The "No-Spin" Zone

iUniverse books may be ordered through booksellers or by contacting:

iUniverse
2021 Pine Lake Road, Suite 100
Lincoln, NE 68512
www.iuniverse.com
1-800-Authors (1-800-288-4677)

ISBN: 978-0-595-43408-4 (pbk)
ISBN: 978-0-595-87732-4 (ebk)

Printed in the United States of America

This book is dedicated
to my late father,
Hardeo Chowthi,
who taught me to
think big.
God bless his soul.

Contents

Author's Note

I suspect that many people who know me personally will probably be surprised or shocked at the tough language I've used against Bill O'Reilly in this book, because I am usually not a judgmental person, and I sure do not like to condemn people and destroy their reputation. Unlike Bill O'Reilly, I understand and appreciate the fact that people will have varying views and different perspectives on things, depending on their life experiences, their beliefs, and their values. Hence, I do not hold it against people that they feel a certain way about a certain issue. People on the left hold certain views about certain subjects, and people on the right hold certain views about certain subjects, because they represent different people and they see things very differently. I further believe that in a free society like the United States of America, everyone has the right to make their views public and fight for what they believe, if they so choose, without fear of being demonized or threatened, as long as they themselves do not advocate violence.

In contrast to Bill O'Reilly, I also do not claim to know and hold the truth to all things, except of course in the usual areas of Mathematics and Science, where things can be proven. In the world of Social Science and Religion, none of us hold the truth, because sometimes there is no truth; we are guided by our conscience and our emotions most of the time, and we cannot *prove* what is *right*. In Mathematics, we all know that two plus two is equal to four, and we can prove it by putting two apples on the table, and then putting another two apples on the table, and merging them together and recounting them. But in Social Science, rarely can we prove anything one way or the other. For example, we cannot prove if a twenty percent tax rate is better than a thirty percent tax rate because there are many issues involved, issues which cannot be easily quantified or which cannot be quantified at all. For a start, it depends on what we mean by "better", and "better" for whom. What is better for one group may not be better for the other group. So when people like Bill O'Reilly comes out and claims to know what's better and claims to know the truth, you have to be skeptical. What he really means is that it is better from a certain perspective, or truthful from a certain perspective, usually his (right-wing) perspective.

The thing that impassioned me to write this book is Bill O'Reilly's intolerance for the views of certain people, and his frequent attempts to assassinate the character of the people he disagrees with, all in the name of being fair and independent. Normally, I am a very diplomatic and tactful person, but in this specific case I believe that in order to fight back against Bill O'Reilly on behalf of the many good people he has smeared and attacked, diplomacy and tactfulness will not work. Fighting back against Bill O'Reilly is one of these rare cases where you have to fight fire with fire. The reason why I think the soft approach will not work with Bill O'Reilly is because I've seen him destroy good people, which is a clear indication that no matter how "nice" you are he will destroy you if he thinks you oppose his ideology or are sympathetic to the Left. One of the things I documented in the book is Bill O'Reilly's vile attack on Pope John Paul II for the Pope's opposition to the Iraq War. If O'Reilly can attack a sinless man like that, what will he do to a sinner like me? So Strap on your seatbelts and prepare for turbulence. The "shoot-out" you are about to witness will probably be the longest and bloodiest you've ever seen, because Bill O'Reilly has finally met his match, or maybe better! Let's give him a taste of his own medicine, for a change. And please forgive me if you find the tone of this book a little harsh, for sometimes there is no other choice but to be harsh. But even though I may be harsh, I have not attacked Bill O'Reilly personally in this book. I have restricted my analysis to his journalistic work, and the bias therein.

Introduction

It seems like no one in the mainstream media, the political establishment, or the academic community is willing or able to systematically confront Bill O'Reilly on his deception and dishonesty, as it relates to his political commentary. Once in a while, someone will offer up some criticism of him, but he would fight back and spin his way out unscathed, because he largely controls the debate most of the time and people do not get a chance to reply. Hence, it is fair to say that so far, he has gone largely uncontested. As a matter of fact, he seems to be getting bolder and bolder every day, destroying the reputations of many very good people, and conning the public into thinking that he is independent, when he is not. He constantly accuses his opponents of being dishonest and unfair, when in fact, he is the main source of dishonesty and unfairness. I have no problem with anyone taking an ideological position and defending that position, or attacking their opponents, as long as they acknowledge their bias one way or the other, or concede that they are coming from a certain ideological or political perspective. I probably would never write a book about Sean Hannity or Rush Limbaugh, for instance, because they are self-described Conservative Republicans, and we know where they are coming from. (Same for Al Franken or Alan Colmes, for example, on the Liberal side). My problem with Bill O'Reilly is that he claims to be fair and independent and says he does not approach issues from an ideological or political perspective, but that is a big lie.

The truth is that Bill O'Reilly is one of the most political journalists in America today, and he is not an independent analyst as he claims. He pushes a particular agenda aimed at promoting right-wing ideas, supporting and defending the Republican Party, and discrediting the Democratic Party and anyone opposed to George W. Bush. His claim to have a "No-Spin" zone is absolutely bogus, and it is just a clever marketing ploy aimed at marketing himself as a fair and independent analyst, when in fact he is one of the biggest peddlers of spin in the mainstream media. He tends to operate the same way a lawyer does: He takes a position and then seeks out arguments to support that position, rather than being objective and following the facts wherever they lead, as a real journalist would do. The purpose of this book is to confront Bill O'Reilly's false claim to be fair and independent, and to expose and critically analyze the methods he employs to promote his right-wing propaganda.

To understand how Bill O'Reilly operates, one has to get an understanding of the concept of PROPAGANDA and how propaganda is employed to influence people's thinking. In my opinion, Bill O'Reilly is one of the most effective users of propaganda in the media today. I have studied him for a long time. I am a regular viewer of *The O'Reilly Factor*, and I have also read all of his books and many of his articles. I see a common theme in nearly everything he says and writes: Republicans and Conservatives are better for America than Democrats and Liberals. This is what seems to guide his thought process as he speaks and writes. And he cleverly assembles his arguments to buttress his ideological position, using certain propaganda techniques that have been proven to work universally over time.

O'Reilly's general method, as I perceive it, is to first set out a theme for each of his presentation, whether on TV or in print, and then employing certain communication techniques or literary devices to artfully deceive the audience and convince them that he is correct on the issue in question, and Democrats and Liberals are wrong. I will systematically go through O'Reilly's methods and techniques step-by-step and back up my arguments with facts and actual quotes from O'Reilly and others where necessary and appropriate. I am not out to assassinate the character of Bill O'Reilly; I am out to prove his bias and deception. There is no one to cut me off or threaten me, so expect full and detailed explanation of every point I make.

1

The Tools Of The Trade

A propagandist, like any other craftsman, utilizes certain tools or instruments to manufacture and refine his product in order to make it into a final salable commodity. In the case of Bill O'Reilly, a master craftsman by any measure, the product is propaganda, and the tools he employs are many and varied. But these tools are not necessarily new. They have been used to control and influence the masses from since the beginning of time, going all the way back to Ancient Rome, to Soviet Russia, to Nazi Germany, and to present day North Korea. To understand how Bill O'Reilly operates and why he has succeeded in his craft thus far, it is essential that one understand these tools and how O'Reilly uses them to manufacture and disseminate the right wing propaganda that emanates from *The O'Reilly Factor* and elsewhere.

1) Omission

Here, O'Reilly deliberately omits information that do not support his argument or do not fit into his theme, with the hope that no one will figure out what has been omitted and he would end up getting away with it. Nine times out of ten, he does get away with it, and hence the propaganda he puts out becomes treated as fact, and people end up believing it. But what people really get is a one sided view of the issue, without realizing it.

He uses omission mainly in two ways. Firstly, he employs omission when making arguments against Democrats and people or groups he disagrees with. For example, one of the groups he has targeted is the ACLU, mainly because it opposes the Bush Administration on many Civil Liberty issues. His main method of attack against the ACLU is to try to label it a "secular" and "anti-spiritual" organization. He knows that the American people are religious, and if he can get them to believe that the ACLU is anti-religious, they will turn against the ACLU and stop supporting it. So what he does is he rehashes the cases pertaining to the *separation of church and state* which the ACLU has been involved with, but **never** mentions the cases that the ACLU has taken on fighting for people's personal religious freedom. The fact is that the ACLU supports religious freedom and has been involved in many cases defending people's right to religious expression, as I point out in Chapter Five. It is an absolute lie to say that the ACLU is secular or anti-religious. I would bet any amount of money that O'Reilly's audience has never heard of the cases where the ACLU has fought for people's religious rights, and so they buy into O'Reilly's propaganda that the ACLU is a secular and anti-spiritual organization, because they are being fed only one angle of the story. I myself was stunned when I did my research and found out that the ACLU has been involved with so many cases standing up for freedom of religion. I was flabbergasted to learn that the ACLU supports students' rights to distribute candy canes with religious messages in school, as well as students' rights to distribute other religious literature in school. I was also very astonished to learn that the ACLU supports conducting baptisms in public parks, and supports people's rights to preach on the public sidewalks. So this notion that the ACLU is against religion and spirituality is absolutely false. I hope that O'Reilly and his supporters read Chapter Five carefully, rethink their position on the ACLU, and cease their nasty attacks on the organization. I say thank God for the ACLU. Had it not been for the ACLU, the United States would have turned into a quasi-police state, where people are afraid to disagree with the government.

Another area in which O'Reilly has employed Omission is in his reporting on former President Bill Clinton. O'Reilly rarely or never reports anything good about President Clinton. A prime example is back in 2001 when O'Reilly wrote an article on Bill Clinton that I think pretty much sums up O'Reilly's method as it relates to Omission. The article appeared in *WorldNetDaily.com* on May 11, 2001 and was titled "The Clinton Legacy." You would expect that an article on President Clinton's legacy would have at least one positive accomplishment of President Clinton, because even the harshest critics of Mr. Clinton would concede that he has done some good to America. But O'Reilly's article did not mention a *single* positive accomplishment of President Clinton. Instead, O'Reilly blamed President Clinton for nearly every problem in America and insinuated that Mr. Clinton was one of the most incompetent and distracted presidents in the history of the Republic. The article was blatantly biased, and I am left to wonder how O'Reilly gets away with stuff like this while there are people out there who still think he is a "no-spin" guy. Check out Chapter Two if you would like to read the article in full and see the kind of garbage O'Reilly puts out as fact. It's incredible, isn't it? There is no mention in the article about poverty rates, economic growth, deficit reduction, or homeownership under President Clinton, just to mention a few major issues where President Clinton was successful. O'Reilly must have a twisted understanding of the term "fair and balanced".

O'Reilly has also failed to report on the good and noble things President Clinton has been involved with since Mr. Clinton left office. So even though Mr. Clinton is no longer President, O'Reilly still treats him unfairly and doesn't want people to know about the good things Mr. Clinton has been up to. O'Reilly doesn't tout the fact that Mr. Clinton, through the Clinton Foundation, has been successful in bringing down the price of drugs used in the treatment of AIDS in Third World countries. The Clinton Foundation negotiated with generic drug manufacturers in South Africa and India that resulted in substantially lower prices for these drugs, thereby giving access to thousands of AIDS patients who would normally not be able to afford the treatment. Many people around the world infected with the AIDS virus are now able to increase their live span due to Mr. Clinton's ingenuity. The results have been remarkable, and this is undoubtedly a tremendous achievement by Mr. Clinton. But O'Reilly has swept it under the rug. Why? It doesn't fit into his agenda, which is to portray Mr. Clinton as a bad and corrupt individual. So O'Reilly prefers to report the issues unfairly, rather than allow his audience to get the true picture.

O'Reilly has done the same thing with former President Jimmy Carter. He has put out only negative things about Mr. Carter (a Democrat also by the way). He has targeted Mr. Carter because Mr. Carter opposes President Bush on many issues, and, as I will note throughout this book, any prominent person who opposes Mr. Bush run the risk of being demonized by O'Reilly. But O'Reilly will have a hard time sliming Mr. Carter, because Mr. Carter is a man of class. Mr. Carter has done some extremely amazing things around the world to help poor and impoverished people, and I think he will go down in history as one of the greatest international statesman ever. Mr. Carter, through the Carter Center based in Atlanta, Georgia, has been involved in promoting democracy in twenty-five countries and has monitored sixty-one elections around the world since 1989. With political parties and factions at each other's throat threatening violence and civil unrest, Mr. Carter has stepped into many situations in some of the most dangerous countries of the world and helped pulled off democratic elections no one thought possible. I can tell you of one such election that I personally followed in Guyana: In 1992 the two main political parties in Guyana would not agree on the procedures and safeguards for conducting the national elections. Many people, both within Guyana and outside of Guyana, never thought that these two parties would ever resolve their differences, and there were fears of civil unrest. But to their credit, the two political parties eventually agreed to allow Mr. Carter to mediate a solution. Mr. Carter succeeded in bringing the parties together and convincing them to accept the proposals set forth by the Carter Center. The result was the first free and fair elections in nearly twenty years in Guyana. And the country has continued to have free and fair elections ever since. It was an amazing accomplishment by Mr. Carter, and the vast majority of the people of Guyana remain thankful to him to this day. This is just one of the many success stories engineered by Mr. Carter, but you would not hear stories such as these on *The O'Reilly Factor* (or on the Fox News Channel for that matter).

Mr. Carter has been involved not only with promoting democracy in the Third World, but he is also involved with economic development and health issues in some of the poorest countries of the world. On the economic front, Mr. Carter has been helping people improve their agricultural techniques so that they can increase their productivity. There is a whole host of initiatives that the Carter Center has funded and supervised, the aim of which is to help people help themselves by getting more from the land they cultivate. The initiatives range from soil preparation all the way to storage of produce, transportation, and marketing. Millions of people have benefited from these initiatives and many lives have been touched one way or the other.

On the health front, Mr. Carter founded the Carter Center's International Disease Control and Prevention Task Force, the purpose of which is to identify and eradicate certain diseases from the Third World. The Task Force targeted Guinea Worm Disease (Dracunculiasis), River Blindness (Onchocerciasis), Lymphatic Filariasis, and Trachoma. Thousands of people have been cured, while many thousands of others were saved from horror due to prevention and education. So when O'Reilly tries to insinuate that Jimmy Carter is a bad person, he (O'Reilly) is either misguided or is being dishonest. You can find out more about Mr. Carter's humanitarian work by logging on to www.cartercenter.org

The second way O'Reilly uses omission is when he wants to take the focus off Republicans and save them from bad publicity or criticism. This happens when there is a scandal or an issue of honesty or competence involving a Republican. O'Reilly would not cover the issue, or would leave out crucial facts in order to try to make the issue dissipate as fast as possible, without causing irreparable damage to the GOP. For example, on the day when the Abramoff scandal broke, and was making headlines everywhere, O'Reilly did not cover the story that evening at all.

That's amazing, isn't it? The next day he dealt with it but in a very restrained manner, very untypical of O'Reilly when it comes to scandal. On the whole, O'Reilly did not churn the Abramoff scandal nearly as much as he churned so-called scandals in the Clinton era. His appetite for confronting corruption in government seems to have waned with the advent of George W. Bush as president. During the Clinton presidency, O'Reilly was calling for investigations practically on a daily basis, wanting everyone investigated from Bill Clinton all the way down to Hillary Clinton, Al Gore, Janet Reno, etc. It's amazing how a change in president has brought about an "evolution" of O'Reilly's attitude towards corruption. We'll see what his attitude will be come 2008 if a Democrat is in the White House.

Because O'Reilly controls everything he puts out on television and print from top to bottom, he has great latitude as to what he can include and what he can exclude. So he uses (and I would argue abuses) that power to the fullest extent possible to achieve his ideological goals. I don't think there is anyone who oversees or edits the garbage he puts out, and he certainly does not have a sense of fairness and independence, so the end result is that the final product he puts out is shaped by his ideology and biases.

2) Selectivity

With selectivity, O'Reilly simply picks and chooses what information he utilizes to make his argument, without regard to fairness or objectivity. When he cannot find solid sources, he tries to win people over to his side of the argument by using questionable data, one sided quotes, incomplete information, etc., as long as the information supports his argument. For example, we all know that President Clinton has also been one of the most popular presidents in the history of the nation. Even during the height of the impeachment trial Mr. Clinton remained highly popular, despite the vicious attacks on him coming from people like Bill O'Reilly. The American people ultimately made the judgment that he is a good man, and when he left office in 2001 he was extremely popular, more so than President Ronald Reagan when he (Mr. Reagan) left office in 1989. And Mr. Clinton continues to be popular to this day. This must really hurt people like Bill O'Reilly bad, and in his desperation to try to prove that Mr. Clinton wasn't a good President, O'Reilly dug up a poll conducted by an academic institution called the Intercollegiate Studies Institute, which he claimed ranked Mr. Clinton among the worst presidents ever to serve.[1] But there is one big, big problem with O'Reilly's poll. Have you ever heard of the Intercollegiate Studies Institute? Many of you may not have, so let me let me tell you who they are. The Intercollegiate College Institute (ISI) is a right-wing academic institution founded by a right-wing ideologue named Frank Chodorov. Chodorov wrote for the right-wing publications Human Events and The National Review. He was regarded as a mentor to Conservative writer William F. Buckley, and he wrote a well know essay called "Taxation is Robbery", in which he basically says that Taxation by the government is robbery, and it is illegal:

> "When the State invades the right of the individual to the products of his labors it appropriates an authority which is contrary to the nature of things and therefore establishes an unethical pattern of behavior, for itself and those upon whom its authority is exerted. Thus, the income tax has made the State a partner in the proceeds of crime; the law cannot distinguish between incomes derived from production and incomes derived from robbery; it has no concern with the source."[2]

The funding for the ISI comes mainly from right-wing individuals such as Richard Mellon Scaife, a multi-millionaire who poured millions of dollars into right-wing media organizations to try to bring Mr. Clinton down in the 1990's. Therefore, a poll from a right-wing organization such as the ISI is simply not credible. I'm frankly not surprised at the dishonesty of O'Reilly in trying to pass this poll off as an impartial survey. He couldn't find a poll to disprove the popularity of Mr. Clinton from the usual polling organizations such as Gallup, Time, Newsweek, or even The Fox News Channel, so he reached for a bogus poll from a right-wing group like the ISI and presented it as a mainstream, non-partisan, independent poll. Does a fair-minded journalist operate like this? I call it desperation. O'Reilly probably suspects that Bill Clinton will go down in history as one of the great presidents, so he is giving it his best shot to try to diminish Mr. Clinton, but it's not going to work. History, I think, will be very kind to Mr. Clinton for the enormous accomplishments he has made both when he was president and after he left office.

O'Reilly often tries his best to demonize Hillary Clinton also on a regular basis because he is terribly worried that she may one day become president. He would like to stop her if he can. So one line of attack he has taken against Mrs. Clinton to try to marginalize her, is to put out the word that she is a big spender, a Socialist, someone who would bust the National Budget and bankrupt the United States. But what is his basis for making this claim? Mrs. Clinton is a smart woman, as we all know. She must have learnt from her husband while he was in office. He didn't bankrupt the United States, quite the contrary, we were heading for a surplus until George W. Bush and his band of ideologues came along and practically emptied the treasury and put the country into debt once again. Mrs. Clinton, if elected president, would most likely follow the footsteps of her husband and ensure that the country follows a sound fiscal policy. Why would she do the opposite when she saw how popular her husband became with his policies? She is not a lunatic. There is no reason to believe that if she is elected president she will run the country much differently from her husband. Chances are she will try to emulate him on fiscal issues. But O'Reilly wants to prove otherwise. So what does he do? He quotes the National Taxpayers Union to back up his argument:

> "First of all, Mrs. Clinton was one of the biggest-spending fresh-man senators in the history of this country, according to the National Taxpayers Union. This organization tracks congress-people's voting records on spending bills, and our pal Hillary voted for just about all of them in her first year. There is no question she wants your money for redistribution under her control."[3]

So who or what is the National Taxpayers Union? Again, it is another blatantly right-wing partisan organization that is against virtually all forms of government spending on the poor. The National Taxpayers Union (NTU) does not look at all spending by politicians, they skew their analysis against Senators and Congresspeople who support spending on the poor; people who spend big on the military or on pork barrel pet projects, for instance, do not get marked down by the NTU. So the NTU is not a neutral organization that looks at spending across the board. Their agenda is to cut social programs as much as possible or eliminate them altogether, so it's no surprise that they would rate Democrats poorly and rate Republicans highly. The NTU was very hostile to Bill Clinton, for example, despite the fact that Mr. Clinton presided over the first balanced budget in many years and left the country in sound fiscal shape. On the other hand they were extremely favorable to President Reagan despite the fact that Mr. Reagan has one of the worse fiscal record in history. (As you may or may not know, under Mr. Reagan's tenure the budget deficit more than doubled, and Mr. Clinton was the one to clean the mess up.) Added to that, they are very favorable to President George W. Bush even though year after year the budget deficit kept getting larger and larger. Do you see the pattern here? And these people have the gall to call themselves a "non-partisan" organization. It's a joke.

But that's not all, the NTU's own rating system doesn't seem to make sense. Even though the deficit increased for 2002, 2003, & 2004, in a *Republican* controlled Senate and a *Republican* controlled House of Representatives, the average ratings of Republicans either went up or remained unchanged:

Year	Average Republican rating (Senate)
2002	62%
2003	73%
2004	71%

Year	Average Republican rating (House)
2002	58%
2003	63%
2004	62%

Source: NTU Website, 2005

How can this be? If Republicans are the majority in both houses, and spending and the deficit keep going up each year, shouldn't the average ratings of Republican Senators and Congresspeople get worse? They didn't. They got *better*. Average Senate Republican rating *rose* from 62% in 2002 to 71% in 2004, and average House Republican rating rose from 58% in 2002 to 62% in 2004. This is totally absurd. What system of rating are these people employing? This undoubtedly demonstrates the partisanship nature of the NTU ratings. It's just a useless set of numbers that are used for political purposes, with no credibility whatsoever. If the ratings were in fact based on Congresspeople's spending actions, the ratings of Republicans should have *fallen* from 2002 to 2004 because spending went through the roof in a Republican dominated House and Senate. So it's clear that the NTU is anti-Democratic and pro-Republican, and statements from this organization cannot be regarded as non-partisan. I am very interested to know where the NTU gets its funding from. I would bet that most of its funding, if not all, comes from people on the Right. So that may explain why they are in bed with the Republicans and constantly slings mud at the Democrats.

O'Reilly also employs Selectivity when quoting from people to buttress his ideological position. He simply cherry picks quotes that support his ideological position and includes them in his arguments and leaves out others that do not support his arguments. Case in point: in Chapter Five of his book *Who's Looking Out for You* he wants to argue that the Founding Fathers favored religion in public and wanted the government to support religion, so he pulls up quotes from Benjamin Franklin, Thomas Jefferson, and James Madison, where these great men expressed their personal faith in God, and used that as the basis for his argument. But what he left out were the statements these great men made about *separation* of church and state. He failed to tell his readers that Jefferson was the one who coined the phrase "wall of separation between church and state" in his famous letter to the Danbury Baptists of Connecticut, and he left out all of Madison's quotes regarding separation of church and state as well as Madison's actions as president that strongly supported separation of church and state. It is true that Franklin, Jefferson, and Madison were religious men, there is no doubt about that, but they did *not* favor *government* involvement in religion. They believed that religion is a private issue and the state must stay out of religion and religious issues. I present the facts to support this in Chapter Six, and when you read Chapter Six, you will see that O'Reilly and his Conservatives friends are wrong about the Founding Fathers' views and beliefs regarding government involvement in religion.

Another instrument O'Reilly employs selectively to support his argument is *polling information*. Whenever there is a poll to support his argument he wouldn't hesitate to inject it into the debate. The aim, I guess, is to say to the opponent "you are on the wrong side" or "the American people are against you". You would think that a moralist like Bill O'Reilly would be more concerned with issues of morality and ethics rather than with public opinion, but sometimes it doesn't appear to be so. When the Iraq War started, for example, O'Reilly was quick to point out that seventy percent of Americans supported the action. He uses the same tactic to back up his argument that the U.S. military should be put on the U.S-Mexican border; he says that over seventy percent of Americans support putting the U.S. military on the southern border. But one category of polling you would not hear O'Reilly talk a lot about these days is polling related to President George W. Bush's honesty and trustworthiness. In most polls where people were asked about Mr. Bush's honesty and trustworthiness, a majority of Americans do not believe he is an honest and trustworthy person. Why don't we hear more about this poll from you, Mr. O'Reilly? You only reference polls when they favor your argument?

The thing that surprises me though is that many times the people debating O'Reilly, especially Democrats, seem not to know how to respond to him when he confronts them with his polls. Democrats need to learn from Republicans.

One thing I admire Republicans for is their guts to sometimes stand up and say that they would do what they think is right rather than go by the polls. Remember President Clinton's impeachment? Republicans didn't care that there was little support for it; they went ahead. So Democrats need to be more steadfast with their convictions; if they feel that something is right or wrong they need to look O'Reilly in the eyes and tell him to stuff his polls.

The other thing they need to tell O'Reilly is that on quite a few major issues the American public has been on the wrong side. For instance, the polls never favored giving equal voting rights to women, or giving equal rights to black people. If politicians went by the polls back then there wouldn't have been any legislation regarding these two important issues. More recently, the public has been on the wrong side of the Iraq War. In 2003 they were overwhelmingly in favor of it, which turned out to be the wrong position. Now that they have seen that it is not going well they are questioning the wisdom of it and have flipped flopped to the point where a majority are now against the war. So politicians cannot make major decisions based on polling, such decisions have to be made based on one's heartfelt convictions and independent, unbiased information. And more importantly, one has to be prepared to stick to those convictions even when polls are showing otherwise.

3) Fabrication

Here, O'Reilly simply makes up his own theory and compiles his own analysis based on whatever he wants to propagate, and then puts it out as if it is fact. Again, in his book *Who's Looking Out for You,* he tries to blame Bill Clinton for the failures of both the FBI and CIA in the wake of the September 11, 2001 tragedy. He constructed two separate theories why he thinks the FBI and the CIA failed to penetrate Al-Qaeda pre 9/11, and you guessed it—Bill Clinton is to be blamed. He basically argued that the FBI failed because Louis Freeh and President Clinton did not talk to each other very much, and the CIA failed because of the so-called "Torreccelli Principle". Both theories are highly nonsensical, and I debunk them both in Chapter Seven. It's just amazing how O'Reilly always seems to *know* exactly what happens whenever the competence of Democrats are in question, even on the most complicated issues, and how he steers the analysis to vilify Democrats.

Back in 2003 when Canada and France did not support the invasion of Iraq, O'Reilly sought revenge against these two countries. He was also angry at Canada for not returning two American Army privates who deserted the United States army and sought refuge in Canada. So he tried to organize a boycott against France, threatened to organize a boycott against Canada, and engaged in a smear campaign against Canada to discredit its government and then Prime Minister Jean Cretien. Regarding Canada, on his December 10, 2003 edition of the O'Reilly Factor he claimed that Canada was a Socialist country that was "nearly" bankrupt:

> "Canada can't help us anyway. They have no military to speak of. And the socialistic system they have there has nearly bankrupted them."

For a start, Canada is not nearly bankrupt, far from it. For the fiscal year 2002 to 2003 Canada posted a surplus of nearly $7 billion, and the forecast for fiscal year 2004 to 2005 was about $3 billion. How did O'Reilly arrive at the idea that Canada was nearly bankrupt? Secondly, O'Reilly's claim that Canada has a Socialist system is likewise unsupported by the facts. Among the G-7 countries, in terms of government spending in proportion to GDP, only Japan and the United States have a lower ratio than Canada. The United Kingdom, Italy, Germany, and France all have higher ratios of government spending to GDP. The Canadian economy was actually quite healthy contrary to what O'Reilly told his viewers. Here are some additional facts about Canada:
—Canada was the only G-7 country to record a surplus in 2002, 2003 and 2004.
—The Organization for Economic Co-operation and Development (OECD) had projected that Canada would be the only G-7 country to record a surplus in both 2005 and 2006.
—Canada has had the largest improvement in its budgetary situation among the G-7 countries since 1992, including the sharpest decline in the debt burden.
—Canada's total government sector debt burden declined to an estimated 31 per cent of gross domestic product (GDP) in 2004, and has been the lowest in the G-7 since 2003.

These are the facts about Canada. O'Reilly was dealing in fabrication, not facts. Canada is not a Socialist country and it is not close to being bankrupt.

Let's move on to France. Just like Canada, O'Reilly constantly blasted France as well for not supporting the Iraq war. He then started a campaign to boycott French goods, which failed, but later claimed that the boycott was working. In his April 27, 2004 "Impact Segment" of *The O'Reilly Factor*, O'Reilly interviewed Heather Mallick of the The Globe and Mail newspaper in Toronto, Canada, and in the interview he threatened to start a boycott against Canada, and warned that it will hurt Canada *just like it hurt France*:

> *O'Reilly*: "… there will be a boycott of your country which will hurt your country enormously. France is now feeling that sting. Because Americans believe that freedom of speech is great. Disagreement we respect, but if you start to undermine our war against terrorists, even if you disagree with it—again, we respect disagreement, if you start to undermine it, then Americans are going to take action. Are you willing to accept that boycott which will hurt your economy drastically?"
>
> *Mallick*: "I don't think for a moment such a boycott would take place because we are your biggest trading partners."
>
> *O'Reilly*: "No, it will take place, Madam. In France …"
>
> *Mallick*: "I don' think that your French boycott has done to well …"
>
> *O'Reilly*: "… they've lost billions of dollars in France according to "The Paris Business" Review."
>
> *Mallick*: "I think that's nonsense."

Well, there is only one problem with O'Reilly's claim that France has lost *billions* due to the boycott—actually, two problems. Firstly, no one seems to know what is "The Paris Business Review". I've done some research but I can't find what publication this is. So we don't know if such a publication exists at all or if O'Reilly was making it up. Hence, the source he quoted was questionable. But even if "The Paris Business Review" does exist, this publication, as well as Bill O'Reilly, was wrong to claim that the boycott against French goods was hurting France, because the trade statistics prove otherwise. Here are the U.S. trade figures with France for 2003 and 2004 taken from the U.S. Census Bureau:

U.S. Imports from France—2003, in millions of U.S. dollars:

January 2003—	2,354.3
February 2003—	2,215.2
March 2003—	2,329.2
April 2003—	2,423.7
May 2003—	2,236.6
June 2003—	2,461.4
July 2003—	2,524.3
August 2003—	2,278.3

September 2003—	2,346.9
October 2003—	2,617.3
November 2003—	2,551.2
December 2003—	2,880.8
Total—	**29,219.3**

U.S. Imports from France—2004, in millions of U.S. dollars:

January 2004—	2,258.0
February 2004—	2,160.8
March 2004—	2,732.3
April 2004—	2,541.9
May 2004—	2,407.1
June 2004—	2,679.7
July 2004—	2,558.2
August 2004—	2,470.8
September 2004—	2,645.6
October 2004—	3,151.8
November 2004—	2,959.5
December 2004—	3,039.9
Total—	**31,605.7**

Source: U.S. Census Bureau

As you can see, France's exports to the United States actually rose from $29.2 billion in 2003 to $31.6 billion in 2004. O'Reilly (and other right-wing groups) called for a boycott against France in the spring of 2003, when France said it was going to vote against the United Nations Resolution authorizing force against Iraq. Even if you look at the month-to-month figures for the second half of 2003 when the boycott was supposed to be in full steam, there is no significant decline in France's exports to the United States. There are month-to-month fluctuations, which are normal, but there is no downward trend to support the claim that French exports to the United States declined during the period in question. So whichever way you look at it, the boycott against France was a failure. Hence, O'Reilly's claim that the boycott against France was working is flat out untrue. Did he get his information from somewhere else or did he just make up his own information?

On March 3, 2005 Bill O'Reilly did a segment on his show relating to Senator Hillary Clinton's job approval rating and her prospects for getting the Democratic Party's nomination for the 2008 presidential elections. His guest was Dick Morris, and O'Reilly began the interview with the following comments to Dick Morris:

> *O'Reilly*: "… I'm a New York State resident and we have the highest taxes in the nation, all right, we have a crumbling infrastructure, we have pension plans for state and city workers out of control, workmen's comp out of control, business leaving the state, upstate New York, worse off than it was before Mrs. Clinton was elected senator, economically, and she's at sixty five percent approval? How is she doing it?"

So let me get this straight, Mr. O'Reilly, Hillary Clinton should be held accountable for the tax rate in New York State? She is also responsible for pension plans and workers comp in the State of New York? She should also be held accountable for businesses moving out of New York State? O'Reilly wanted to give his listeners the impression that Hillary Clinton has been a failure, so he piles up all of the problems facing New York State and insinuates that Hillary Clinton hasn't really done anything for the State, and he's shocked that sixty five percent of New Yorkers approve of her job. I'm surprised that he didn't blame 9/11 on Senator Clinton too. But the fact is that Hillary Clinton, as a Senator, has nothing to do with the tax rate in the State of New York, that's the State Legislature and the Governor's responsibility. If O'Reilly thinks that the tax rate in New York State is too high he ought to blame it on them, not on Hillary Clinton. Same for State and City pension plans and workers comp. The truth is that a U.S. Senator really has no control over state and local laws or decisions. A Senator can fight for funds from the Federal Government for his or her state, but that's just about it. O'Reilly is a bright man who holds a Master Degree from Harvard's Kennedy School of Government, so I find it hard to believe that he hasn't read Article 1, Section 8 of the United States Constitution which details the power of Congress. He should know what U.S. Senators do; so my conclusion is that he probably deliberately misrepresented the situation to try to make Senator Clinton look bad. But it didn't work.

You would think that Dick Morris would have corrected O'Reilly, wouldn't you? I say so because the Clintons were the ones who practically made Dick Morris into a national figure, and if he had an ounce of loyalty in little finger he would have tried to set the record straight. To my knowledge, Morris has not said that the Clintons wronged him in any way, so my only conclusion is that he turned against the Clintons because that gave him a better opportunity to make money. He probably thought that there is no money to be made by remaining loyal to the Clintons, so he teamed up with the right-wing and joined in with the Clinton bashing. And it paid off big time. He ended up making a lot of money writing books and doing television appearances trashing the Clintons. This is the type of guy O'Reilly hangs out with.

4) Demonization, Repetition, Association and Diversion

I grouped these four concepts together because they are often used as a *package* by O'Reilly to tear down his opponents and tarnish their reputation without having to deal with the substance of the issues. Here O'Reilly does not engage in philosophical debate, but instead:
—Calls people names, applies labels to them, and talk about them in sarcastic and scornful terms.
—Constantly repeats the name calling and labeling to try to get them to stick.
—Uses the labels to associate people with other people or concepts that are not popular.
—In the process, diverts from the main issue and thrashes his opponents without really dealing with the issue at hand.

O'Reilly's most popular terms these days are "far left", "off the chart far left", "far left ideologues", "far left radical", "left wing loon", "socialist" and "secular progressives". You would hardly find a segment of *The O'Reilly Factor* these days where O'Reilly has not used these terms or something similar. In a way, these words have become trademark O'Reilly terms, because they are not used nearly as much by other people as O'Reilly uses them. I suspect he has done a focus group or he has seen some type of polling information where these words evoke negative impressions, and that is what I think drives him to frequently use these terms. He is a very astute communication expert who should never be underestimated.

I suspect that he slaps these labels on people he wants to demonize because he feels that he cannot win by sticking to the issues. One of the areas where he has ratcheted up the personal attacks is the Iraq War. He has become increasingly desperate because the initial reasons for the war can no longer be justified, and the execution of the war has become a disaster. So defending the war is difficult, and the only way to win the argument seems to be to attack the opponents of the war. Hence, we have his nasty attacks on people like Cindy Sheehan, Michael Moore, and others. On a little side note, it's interesting when he was debating Michael Moore during the 2004 DNC convention coverage and Michael Moore asked him if he would send his kid to fight in Iraq he would not say yes. That tells you something, doesn't it? O'Reilly constantly claims that we are engaged in World War III, but yet he is not willing to send his kid to fight but wants other people's kids to do the fighting.

He also uses Demonization quite effectively when reporting on people like George Soros and others who support Liberal causes. As Americans, we all know that it is our right to support whatever political ideology we choose, as long as it does not involve or promote violence. But O'Reilly wants the American public to believe that Soros and others like him are doing something wrong by financially supporting groups that promote Liberal ideas. O'Reilly however does not zero in on wealthy individuals on the Right who pour money into right-wing causes (like Richard Mellon Scaife, for example—which I deal with in Chapter Two) and say that they are doing anything wrong, but he demonizes Soros to the extent of personally attacking the man. O'Reilly has insulted Soros and called him all sorts of derogatory names in an attempt to portray him as an evil human being who's out to bring harm to America. I have no doubt that O'Reilly probably believes in his heart that Soros is an evil person, but does that give O'Reilly the right to malign Soros the way he has? Think of it, if we all behave like O'Reilly, what do you think will happen to our public discourse? If other Conservatives carry on like O'Reilly, and Liberals follow suit, the atmosphere will become so poisoned that nothing will get done. O'Reilly certainly is not an example that anyone wants to follow.

Apart from slapping labels to people, O'Reilly also denigrates people he disagrees with by misrepresenting their positions and talking about them in derogatory terms. He puts out the worst possible description of someone and tries to paint him or her as an evil person. Once again, in his book *Who's Looking Out for You*, he preemptively strikes at the prospect of Hillary Clinton becoming president by saying "If President Hillary becomes a reality, the United States will be a polarized, thief-ridden nanny state with a mean-spirited headliner living on Pennsylvania Avenue."[4] Pretty pathetic, isn't it? You would think that for someone who attended Harvard the debate would have some intellectual depth to it rather than being so shallow.

Now we come to the name-calling, which is major part of the demonization process. Here, the debate (if you want to call it that) is even more shallow and pathetic. You would expect to hear this level of discourse in the playground of an elementary school, not on the number one cable television prime time show in America. People are called "nut", "crazy", "fanatic", "loon", and other derogatory names on a routine basis. Even the word "bum" is sometimes used to try to demean people. And to add insult to injury, O'Reilly frequently lashes out at the "left wing smear merchants" for besmirching people they disagree with. It's time for you to look yourself in the mirror, Mr. O'Reilly; you are the number one smear merchant is America, Sir. Here are just a few examples of some of the name-calling you've engaged in, in you own words, that were totally unwarranted. I could probably fill half of this book with stuff like this, but there are too many other things to get to and I'm hard pressed for space:

—On George Soros: "George Soros, another far-left **fanatic**". (The O'Reilly Factor, January 6, 2006).

—On George Soros: "So far, Left wing **loon** George Soros has given nearly $24 million to help John Kerry." (The O'Reilly Factor, October 29, 2004).

—On Nancy Peloci: "She's a **nut**. I'm not—I don't care what she says. She's a **fanatic**." (The Radio Factor with Bill O'Reilly, July 21, 2004).

—On Barbara Streisand: "If you look at her website, she is kind of **crazy**." (The O'Reilly Factor, March 29, 2006).

—On David Letterman: "There is no question he lives in the **left-wing** precincts." (The O'Reilly Factor, October 31, 2006).

—On Jacques Chirac and Jean Cretien: "Pardon me as I object to the anti-American foreign press and **bums** like Chirac in France and Cretien in Canada." (The O'Reilly Factor, July 9, 2004).

It is amazing and sickening not only that the Fox News Channel has someone on the air with this type of vocabulary, but that they seem to be proud of it. And what's even more sickening is the fact that O'Reilly's followers think that he is a great guy. These people must all have a deranged view of the notion of fairness and decency.

O'Reilly uses the instrument of *Repetition* to hammer home certain points that are not necessarily true, in an attempt to have the public believe them, or to support an argument that he is trying to make. The idea is to repeat something often enough so that people come to accept it. For example, he constantly, constantly uses the phrase "the Bush Haters" or the "Bush Hating Press" in order to evoke sympathy for George W. Bush, and to convey the notion that there are people out there working against President Bush. Now I am not denying that there are people who do not like President Bush and want to see him fail, but that's the way it has always been with U.S. Presidents—there is always a section of society (media, academia, etc.) that does not like the president in power because they are from the opposing political ideology. It was the same thing, or even worse, when Bill Clinton was president. The hatred for Mr. Clinton was extremely intense in some circles of the media and academia. President Clinton was accused of being a murder and a rapist by some in the right-wing media, remember? So it is nothing new that a section of Americans dislike President Bush, this is the way it will always be, because we have two political parties with opposing ideology. If Al Gore was President, believe me, the hatred for him would have probably been more intense that what President Bush is experiencing. So O'Reilly is just spinning this to try to demonize the people who oppose President Bush.

Another term O'Reilly repeats endlessly is "far left". If you go back to his television show *The O'Reilly Factor* and see how many times he has used the term "far left" in each edition you will be amazed at the repetitiousness. The idea is to work people's emotions up and constantly remind them of the left wing forces in the country. Yet another phrase he uses very often to lash out at people who scrutinize and criticize him is "far left smear websites". He wants his viewers to think that the Right does not have smear websites, or that the smear websites on the Left are much more vicious than smear websites on the Right, but of course neither of that is true. The right-wing websites are more plenty and far more vicious. If you don't believe me, wait for 2008, especially if Hillary Clinton is the Democratic Party nominee for president, and you will see what I mean.

Parallel to *Demonization* and *Repetition* is the technique of *Associating* his opponents with people he deems unworthy. This is like a form of *guilt by association*. For example, when Cindy Sheehan first started her war protests, O'Reilly went on the offensive, linking her to Michael Moore, The Fenton Group, and other so-called "far left" organization. He wasn't interested in the substance of the debate. All he was interested in was to put her in the company of certain people and slap a label on all of them. But we all know what's going on here. People who have common interests (like Cindy Sheehan and Michael Moore) are bound to be friendly to each other and communicate with each other about one thing or another. What's wrong with that? Groups on the Right do the same. In the Bill Clinton era the right-wing attack groups were all connected in some way or the other. O'Reilly himself is associated with some unsavory characters, such as Dick Morris. Should we paint O'Reilly with the same brush as Dick Morris because they are in the same company? Is it fair to associate people the way O'Reilly does? I don't believe so.

In Chapter Three of O'Reilly's book *Who's Looking Out for You*, he links Gary Winnick, CEO of the failed telecommunications company Global Crossing, to Bill Clinton in this way: He introduced the story by first saying that on *Mr. Clinton's* watch the company went bankrupt and resulted in millions of people losing their investment. Then he went on to say that Clinton's best friend, Terry McAuliffe, had invested in Global Crossing and made millions before the company went bankrupt, and all that while Winnick got to play golf and hang out with President Clinton. So Bill Clinton really didn't do anything wrong or illegal in the grand scheme of things here, but O'Reilly threw him in there with Winnick anyway to try to tarnish his reputation. (What the hell, taint Bill Clinton, right? Why not?)

On the other side of the aisle, O'Reilly treats Republicans differently, and this is what makes me mad. If O'Reilly applied the same level of contempt to Republicans when dubious things happening on their side I will have no quarrel. Contrast the Gary Winnick story above with the Enron scandal that occurred on President George W. Bush's watch. Kenneth Lay, founder and ex-chairman of Enron, was a close friend of President George W. Bush (as well as George H.W. Bush), but O'Reilly does not associate Bush with Lay and does not try to make Bush look like a crook because of his association with Lay. Do you see what I mean? Likewise, Ted Haggard, the disgraced evangelist from Colorado was an adviser to President George W. Bush, but O'Reilly does not make any connection between Haggard's immoral conduct and Bush's character. I'm not saying that O'Reilly should make any connection in either of these two situations concerning President George W. Bush. What I am saying is that in the case of a Democrat (Bill Clinton), he doesn't have any qualms about making connections, but with a Republican (George W. Bush), he stops short of doing so. So what does this tell you about O'Reilly's claim to be fair and independent?

Finally, we come to *Diversion*. Here, O'Reilly skillfully diverts from the main issue and pursues a tangential issue while appearing to still deal with the main issue. This is required when he believes that the main issue will hurt the Republican in question, and he wants to give the audience the impression that he is debating the issue, but really he is not. One method of diversion is to personally attack the people he disagrees with instead of engaging in debate on the issue in question. For example, whenever opposition to the Iraq War surfaces, he segues into his "anti-Bush" mantra and lashes out against the war opponents and blames everyone else, rather than holding President Bush accountable for the chaos.

When the wire tapping issue broke and questions were raised about the legality of President Bush's actions, rather than seeking to find out if the President broke the law or not, O'Reilly went on the attack and crucified the people who argued that the President did break the law. One such person was Newsweek columnist Jonathan Alter who wrote an article critical of the President's action. But Alter went a stage further and said that President Bush *knew* that he was breaking the law. O'Reilly seized upon this immediately and made Jonathan Alter the issue. He blasted Alter for saying that President Bush "knew" that he was breaking the law, and invited Presidential Historian Douglas Brinkley for a whole segment to talk about Jonathan Alter. He tried his best to lure Mr. Brinkley into saying bad things about Alter, but Brinkley did not fall for the trap and was very diplomatic about Alter. O'Reilly nevertheless continued his attack on Alter without dealing with the issue of whether President Bush broke the law or not.[5] I doubt that anyone listening that day learnt anything about the wire tapping issue. So the whole exercise was just a diversion from the main issue, which was probably O'Reilly's intention right from the beginning.

5) Oversimplification

O'Reilly applies *Oversimplification* when attacking his opponents for not doing enough or for failure to deliver results. What he does here is oversimplify the issue and give the audience the impression that there was an easy solution but the person in question was either incompetent, distracted, or corrupt (usually a Democrat). Of course, many times this is not the case, because if things were as easy as O'Reilly makes them out to be, then Republicans would have had them done and solved all the problems, wouldn't they? Here is a prime example of his oversimplification: one of the accusations he makes against President Clinton in his Book *Who's Looking Out for You* is that "on his watch Al-Qaeda grew in ferocity and power". O'Reilly did not get into the issue in depth to try to find out what the Clinton Administration did to fight Al-Qaeda at the time and the context within which the administration had to work. Instead, he oversimplifies the issue by saying that since Al-Qaeda struck nine months after Mr. Clinton left office it is fair to say that Mr. Clinton did not do much or anything to try to neutralize the terrorist organization. But that is an intellectually dishonest piece of analysis on the part of O'Reilly, in my opinion, and it fits into his pattern of trying to always blame Mr. Clinton and tarnish his reputation. The Clinton Administration did do a lot to try to degrade Al-Qaeda prior to Mr. Clinton leaving office, but was constrained by other factors at the time. Mr. Clinton did not have the goodwill that President George W. Bush received after September 11, 2001, so it was difficult for Mr. Clinton to do what President Bush did in Afghanistan. I present a fair and balanced analysis of this issue in Chapter Eight.

O'Reilly is always careful though not to apply oversimplification when dealing with George W. Bush and Republicans. He is often more analytical and accommodating when dealing with GOP failures. You don't hear O'Reilly blaming the Bush Administration for the nuclear threats emanating from North Korea and Iran, and criticizing Mr. Bush for not doing more to stop these two nations from getting nuclear weapons. But he sure blames Bill Clinton for the North Korea nuclear threat. In his Book *Who's Looking Out for You*, page 60, he identified North Korea as one of Mr. Clinton's failures, by oversimplifying the issues and pontificating that "During Mr. Clinton's administration North Korea cheated on a nuclear treaty brokered by the U.S.A., and now we're facing a serious problem". O'Reilly did not say what he thinks should have been done nor does he have any solution to the problem, but he is eager to blame Mr. Clinton. Six years have passed and the Bush administration has done practically nothing to diffuse the situation, but O'Reilly is not yet ready to cast blame on Mr. Bush. Neither does he blame President Bush for the mess in Iraq; instead he focuses on the opponents of the Iraq war and blasts them for "having no solution", as if they are the ones who started the war. So it is clear that he applies his oversimplification very selectively, with a clear ideological goal in mind.

Hurricane Katrina is another issue where O'Reilly has been soft on President Bush, in contrast to how he has dealt with Bill Clinton on similar issues. Mr. Bush is the head of the Federal Government, isn't he? So why didn't O'Reilly hold him accountable for the failure of the federal government to respond effectively? In his Talking Points Memo of September 6, 2005, O'Reilly admits that "once the levees were breached, the situation became a national security issue, and the feds should have arrived in force," but he goes on to say "I don't know why President Bush and Michael Chertoff didn't just seize control." That's it? O'Reilly just doesn't know why President Bush didn't seize control? Why didn't you ask Mr. Bush, Mr. O'Reilly? Or how about calling Mr. Bush "incompetent", Mr. O'Reilly? You don't want to make Mr. Bush look bad, do you? So you rather leave it at that. I understand. But would you treat a Democrat the same way? I don't think so. You would have demanded an investigation and created a huge uproar. Fair and Balanced, do you think?

Another issue he has oversimplified and blamed Bill Clinton for is corporate corruption, and here is how he framed the issue:

"On his watch, corruption in the corporate world escalated until it exploded into scandal because law enforcement under Attorney General Reno was so lax."[6]

So I guess this is O'Reilly's explanation of corporate scandals like Enron, Tyco, etc. But we all know that the issue is not so simple. The Justice Department cannot monitor the books of corporation. If they do that O'Reilly will probably be the first one to accuse the government of overreaching. America is a big country with lots of corporations, and there is no way the federal government can police all of these corporations to make sure greedy or incompetent executives are not screwing things up. How can you blame President Clinton for corporate scandals? It's absurd.

6) Double Standard

Plain old *Double Standard* is probably O'Reilly's most widely used instrument in television as well as print. He just changes the standard, the tone, and the rhetoric accordingly depending on whom he is talking about and what he wants to convey, so that the audience will be influenced accordingly. In dealing with Democrats and people he doesn't like, the standard is strict, the tone is rough, and the rhetoric is harsh. He employs black and white standards of honesty and integrity and confronts his adversaries head-on in an attempt to show that they are dishonest, incompetent or incorrect. But in dealing with Republicans and people sympathetic to his ideology, he pulls back, and applies a whole different set of standards with a softer tone.

For example, there have been some major GOP scandals in the last session of Congress but yet none are on O'Reilly's radar screen. He chose not to bring these issues under the microscope as he did when Democrats were in charge and accused of wrong doings. The case of Tom DeLay is a classic example. Despite the fact that Tom DeLay has been embroiled in all sorts of ethics issues, and has been reprimanded by the House Ethics Committee, O'Reilly chose NOT to blast him or denigrate him in any way. Had this been a Democrat, O'Reilly would have gone on his nightly rampage and shred him to pieces. Then there is the Abramoff scandal, and the Duke Cunningham scandal, but where is O'Reilly? Where is Mr. Ethics? I'm sure his viewers don't know the full story surrounding these GOP scandals, because O'Reilly didn't bother to explain them in a way ordinary people can understand, something he doesn't fail to do when Democrats are involved.

Sometimes O'Reilly even tries to fog up the alleged wrong doings committed by Republicans to give his viewers the impression that the allegations are murky and not real. He also reminds his viewers that the people involved (Republicans) are innocent until proven guilty, something he doesn't do when talking about Democrats suspected of wrongdoing. When he dealt with the Tom DeLay and Jack Abramoff scandals he did not make any attempt to methodically go through the allegations and present them in a way that ordinary people can understand. O'Reilly is usually very meticulous and down-to-earth when explaining issues to his audiences. Remember the Clinton years? O'Reilly would go through each allegation step by step and break it down for the audience. But in the case of DeLay and Abramoff he pretended that he didn't understand the allegations and that it was difficult to explain it all to the public. The end result was that his audience probably didn't get a good understanding of the alleged misdeeds of the Republicans involved. (Please see Chapter Two if you would like to get an easy understanding of the allegations surrounding Tom DeLay.)

Another example of O'Reilly's double standard is his changing attitude towards presidential interviews. I can never forget O'Reilly blasting Jim Lehrer for not hammering President Clinton on the Monica Lewinsky scandal during an interview Mr. Lehrer did with Mr. Clinton at the height of the Monica Lewinsky scandal. O'Reilly chided Jim Lehrer for not being tough on Mr. Clinton and not insisting on clear and complete answers. But when O'Reilly's time came to interview President George W. Bush, he said that interviews with Presidents are special, and one must behave respectfully. In O'Reilly's own words, "Now interviewing a president is not like interviewing anyone else on the planet. You cannot be confrontational with the president of the United States. You can be direct, but you can't be disrespectful."[7] So clearly O'Reilly applies different standards depending on which party the President comes from. With a Republican president he is prepared to be "respectful", but with a Democratic president he insists on clear and complete answers. So it is clear that in O'Reilly's world the treatment and coverage of a Democratic President is different from that of a Republican President, which now brings me to presidential pardons.

O'Reilly made a huge stink about President Clinton's pardon of Marc Rich and said that the pardon of Marc Rich *proves* that Mr. Clinton is a corrupt man:

> "Although I still wish Clinton good tidings, I continue to believe he is a corrupt man. Prove me wrong Mr. Clinton—Reveal the facts about the Marc Rich pardon and the campaign finance shenanigans!"[8]

Well, let's deal with the facts. The fact is that Mr. Clinton has answered ALL questions related to his pardoning of Marc Rich. Unlike other presidents before him who have granted controversial pardons (including Ronald Reagan and George H. W. Bush), Mr. Clinton has issued a thorough statement outlining his reasons for pardoning Marc Rich. On February 18, 2001 Mr. Clinton wrote an Op-Ed piece in the New York Times spelling out eight reasons why he pardoned Mr. Rich. Such detailed explanation by a president on this topic is unprecedented in American history. Yet, O'Reilly continues to mislead his audience by telling them that Mr. Clinton has not revealed the facts about the pardon, and that he issued the pardon for corrupt reasons. I suspect O'Reilly does not agree with the facts so he ignores them and continues to deceive the public. An extremely important fact O'Reilly has hidden from his viewers is the fact that Mr. Clinton granted the pardon to Mr. Rich on the condition that he (Mr. Rich) waive all defenses, including statute of limitations defenses, to any *civil* charges the U.S. government might subsequently bring against him. Before granting the pardon, Mr. Clinton requested and received a letter from Mr. Rich's attorney confirming that Mr. Rich "waives any and all defenses which could be raised to the lawful imposition of civil fines or penalties in connection with the actions and transactions alleged in the indictment against him in the Southern District of New York." What this means is that Mr. Rich is still open to financial liability for his alleged swindling of the U.S. government, and the government can go after him in a *civil case* to recover any and all monies the courts deem outstanding. So Mr. Rich is clearly not off the hook. Should be return to the United States the government can sue him civilly and he will have to pay every cent he owes should he lose the case. The Clinton pardon in effect shifted the proceedings from a criminal proceeding to a civil proceeding; Mr. Clinton did not wipe the slate clean for Mr. Rich.

What I object to here is the fact that Bill O'Reilly singled out Mr. Clinton for criticism on pardons. He did not scrutinize or criticize President George H. W. Bush or President Ronald Reagan for their pardons. President Bush (Sr.) pardoned former Defense Secretary Casper Weinberger who was indicted for obstructing Congress, in the Iran-Contra affair. One can argue that the main reason for President Bush's pardon was to protect himself, because had the investigation and trial of Casper Weinberger proceeded, it was likely that damning testimony against Mr. Bush Sr. would have come out. Weinberger could have possibly ended up testifying against Mr. Bush Sr. By pardoning Weinberger Mr. Bush effectively ended the investigations and prevented further testimony from coming out. So what say you, Mr. O'Reilly? What is your opinion on this one? Is

President George H. W. Bush a corrupt man also? Why didn't you address this when you dealt with Mr. Clinton's pardoning of Marc Rich? Being a bit selective, are you?

Or how about taking a look at President Reagan's pardoning of George Steinbrenner? Steinbrenner was fined $15,000.00 in 1972 for "conspiring to violate federal election laws by making corporate contributions to Richard M. Nixon's 1972 presidential re-election campaign." So here you had a financial contributor to the Republican Party, who was pardoned by President Reagan (in his second term). Is this okay, Mr. O'Reilly? How come you are not passing judgment on a case like this? Why scrutinize only a President who is a Democrat?

Getting back to the Marc Rich pardon, O'Reilly tried to make the case that Mr. Clinton's *only* motivation was the financial donation that came from Marc Rich's ex wife, Denise Rich. But as we learnt later, Mr. Clinton identified eight reasons why he granted the pardon. For a full text of Mr. Clinton's Op-Ed piece please see Appendix 1A. One of the main reasons for the pardon, according to Mr. Clinton, was that he wanted to do a favor to former Israeli Prime Minister Ehud Barak and other Jewish leaders. They requested and supported the pardon because Marc Rich was involved in many charitable causes in Israel, and was also involved with the Israeli's intelligence services (The Mossad) in helping to evacuate Jews from hostile countries. President Clinton did discuss the pardon with Mr. Barak and there are transcripts to prove this. When congress was investigating the issue, Rep Dan Burton, Republican chairman of the House Government Reform Committee, and no friend of Mr. Clinton, released transcripts of telephone conversations between Mr. Clinton and Mr. Barak where, among other things, Mr. Clinton expressed his concern that the pardon might be controversial. So this notion that financial contributions from Denise Rich was the driving force behind the pardon is absolutely slanderous. O'Reilly is wrong to claim that Mr. Clinton issued the pardon for corrupt reasons.

We all know about O'Reilly's feelings towards Democrats such as Bill Clinton, Hillary Clinton, Al Gore, Janet Reno, Jessie Jackson, etc. as it relates to honesty and integrity. There is no doubt that he feels that these people are corrupt and dishonest, as evidenced by the many negative columns and television segments he has done on them. So let's turn the focus a little to the current president, President George W. Bush, a Republican. Surprise, Surprise, O'Reilly thinks President George W. Bush is honest!!

"Summing up, I believe George W. Bush is personally honest …"[9]

What is the difference between "honest" and "personally honest"? Anyone? I'm not sure what is O'Reilly's point when he throws in the word "personally". Come on O'Reilly let's have some straight talk. Either someone is honest or they're not honest. I will take it that he is saying that George W. Bush is an honest man. No spin.

Is George W. Bush an honest man? Well, as one television network likes to say, I report, you decide:

Item:

In Bob Woodward's book *"Plan Of Attack"* he documents a meeting that took place on the morning of Saturday December 21, 2002 in the oval office involving President Bush and other members of his Administration. If Woodward's account is true, then I think it raises some serious questions, and we deserve an explanation from President Bush. According to Woodward, George Tenet, the then Director of the CIA, and John McLaughlin, the then Deputy Director of the CIA, headed over to the White House to present the "Case" on Iraq's Weapons of Mass Destruction to the President, the Vice President, Condoleezza Rice, and Andy Card. After the presentation the President was not impressed. I quote:

> "When McLaughlin concluded, there was a look on the president's face of, What's this? And then a brief moment of silence.
> 'Nice try,' Bush said. 'I don't think this is quite—it's not something that Joe Public would understand or would gain a lot of confidence from."
> Card was also underwhelmed. The presentation was a flop. In terms of marketing, the examples didn't work, the charts didn't work, the photos were not gripping, the intercepts were less than compelling.
> Bush turned to Tenet. 'I've been told all this intelligence about having WMD and this is the best we've got?'
> From the end of one of the couches in the Oval Office, Tenet rose up, threw his arms in the air. 'It's a slam dunk case!' the DCI said.
> Bush pressed. 'George, how confident are you?'
> Tenet, a basketball fan who attended as many home games of his alma mater Georgetown as possible, leaned forward and threw up his arms again. 'Don't worry, it's a slam dunk!'
> It was unusual for Tenet to be so certain. From McLaughlin's presentation, Card was worried that there might be no 'there there,' but Tenet's double reassurance on the slam-dunk was both memorable and comforting. Cheney could think of no reason to question Tenet's assertion. He was after all, the head of the CIA and would know the most. The president later recalled that McLaughlin's presentation 'wouldn't have stood the test of time,' but Tenet's reassurance, 'that was very important.'

'Needs a lot more work,' Bush told Card and Rice. 'Let's get some people who've actually put together a case for a jury.' He wanted some lawyers, prosecutors if need be. They were going to have to go public with something.
The president told Tenet several times, 'Make sure no one stretches to make our case.'"[10]

In order to fully appreciate the gravity and importance of the moment above, I would like you, the reader, to put yourself in the President's position for a moment. Imagine that you were in that meeting and you came to the same conclusion as the President, i.e. you weren't impressed with the evidence being presented, which was clearly the case, based on what Woodward writes. Would you have come out telling the public that you're convinced that Iraq possessed Weapons of Mass Destruction? Would you? I don't think any honest person would, because the fact is that the evidence wasn't strong as presented by the Director of the CIA, and President Bush admits so in the meeting, according to Woodward's reporting. Bush said "I've been told all this intelligence about having WMD and this is the best we've got?" I would assume that the most top secrets were presented at that meeting and nothing was held back. So when Tenet told the President "It's a slam dunk", they must have been talking about everything that was presented at that meeting.

Tenet told Mr. Bush twice that "It's a slam dunk", but is that good enough? If say you're a jury judging a case, and the evidence being presented is not strong and convincing, but the prosecutor kept saying "The evidence is strong", would you convict based on the words of the prosecutor—"The evidence is strong"? Here is the President of the United States making a decision about war and peace, sending our sons and daughters to war, and did so based on evidence that was not convincing to him. But that's not all. In his State of the Union speech of January 28, 2003, just over a month after being presented with the evidence against Iraq by the Director of the CIA and concluding that the evidence wasn't convincing, President Bush told America and the world the following:

"The United Nations concluded in 1999 that Saddam Hussein had biological weapons materials sufficient to produce over 25,000 liters of anthrax; enough doses to kill several million people. He hasn't accounted for that material. He has given no evidence that he has destroyed it.
The United Nations concluded in 1999 that Saddam Hussein had materials sufficient to produce more than 38,000 liters of botulinum toxin; enough to subject millions of people to death by respiratory failure. He hasn't accounted for that material. He's given no evidence that he has destroyed it.

Our intelligence officials estimate that Saddam Hussein had the materials to produce as much as 500 tons of sarin, mustard and VX nerve agent. In such quantities, these chemical agents could also kill untold thousands. He's not accounted for these materials. He has given no evidence that he has destroyed them.

U.S. Intelligence indicates that Saddam Hussein had upwards of 30,000 munitions capable of delivering chemical agents. Inspectors recently turned up 16 of them, despite Iraq's recent declaration denying their existence. Saddam Hussein has not accounted for the remaining 29,984 of these prohibited munitions. He has given no evidence that he has destroyed them …

The International Atomic Energy Agency confirmed in the 1990's that Saddam Hussein had an advanced nuclear weapons development program, had a design for a nuclear weapon and was working on five different methods of enriching uranium for a bomb."

Is this the same man who wasn't impressed by the evidence presented to him by his own intelligence services just over a month ago? What changed from December 21, 2002 to January 29, 2003? The answer is nothing changed. No new evidence was unearthed. How could someone claim to be honest when he was told that something is a certain way but tells everyone else that it's a different way? This is what the President did. He saw the evidence on WMD's, wasn't convinced, but told everyone else that the evidence was strong. Does this raise any questions at all about Mr. Bush's honesty, Mr. O'Reilly? Would you care to comment? Sir?

Item:

As of the time of writing this book, George W. Bush has not revealed the truth about his military service record and how he managed to jump ahead of thousands on a waiting list and secure a spot in the Texas Air National Guard. There are really two issues of veracity here: one is we still don't know whether George W. Bush fulfilled his obligations as required when he enlisted in the Guard, and the other is how he jumped ahead of thousands of other young men and gained entrance into the Guard in the first place, and thereby avoid being drafted to go to Vietnam. We don't know the truthful answer to any of these questions because the President wouldn't tell us.

Let's deal with the latter issue first. According to published reports, George W. Bush enlisted in the Texas Air National Guard on May 27, 1968, which was just days before he graduated from Yale University. Had he not enlisted he would have become eligible for the draft, and once drafted he would not have been able to enlist for the Texas Air National Guard, and could have been sent into combat in Vietnam. So the timing was well calculated to dodge the draft, and unlike John Kerry who volunteered to go to Vietnam, George W. Bush chose the Texas Air National Guard route and avoided being drafted to go to Vietnam. But the key question here is how did he get into the Guard given that approximately one hundred thousand young men had signed up before him and were waiting to be called. Mr. Bush says he got no preferential treatment. And Bill O'Reilly tells us that Mr. Bush is an honest man? Well, I am from Mars. But seriously, telling someone that you got no preferential treatment when in fact you were able to bypass one hundred thousand human beings who were in front of you is simply not credible, just not credible. But O'Reilly is willing to give Mr. Bush a pass. In this case honesty doesn't seem to matter, and despite Mr. Bush's unbelievable answer, O'Reilly still says Mr. Bush is an honest man.

Based on investigations by the various media organizations, it is believed that George W. Bush got into the Texas Air National Guard through the following means: Bush's father, George H.W. Bush was a congressman in Houston, Texas, when George W. Bush was admitted to the Texas Air National Guard in May of 1968. Former Texas House speaker and Lieutenant Governor, Ben Barnes, (a Republican by the way) said in a sworn affidavit that he pulled strings on behalf of the Bush family to get George W. Bush into the Texas Air National Guard. Barnes was supposedly contacted by Houston businessman Sidney Adger, a very close friend of George H. W. Bush and someone known throughout Texas as a longtime and well connected Bush associate. So it is believed that Bush Sr. had Adger contact Barnes who pulled the strings and got Bush Jr. into the Guard. Adger, by the way, also got his two sons into the same Texas Guard Unit, according to published reports. So George W. Bush's claim that he didn't get any preferential treatment doesn't seem to be true. But yet O'Reilly, the man who claims to have contempt for people who do not tell the truth, embraces Mr. Bush. In fact, O'Reilly allowed Mr. Bush to spin the issue in his softball interview of him in 2004, and didn't challenge Mr. Bush at all on the answers he gave. Mr. Bush made the absurd statement that if he got preferential treatment he wasn't aware of it, in effect saying he had no clue what was going on:

> *O'Reilly:* "... All right, do you think you got any preferential treatment getting into the Air Guard during Vietnam?"
> *Bush:* "No. I don't. As a matter of fact, the General that, or the commander of the unit Buck Staudt, said, said the same thing. No."
> *O'Reilly:* "So you don't think you got any preferential treatment because you were a Bush?"

Bush: "I don't. If I did, I have, I'm not,—I'm not aware of it, and again, the, commander of my unit, Buck Staudt, said the other day, publicly, I got no preferential treatment."

So the defense is basically, one, even if I got preferential treatment I wasn't aware of it, and two, the Commander of my unit Buck Staudt said that I didn't get any preferential treatment.

The first defense is totally ridiculous and just adds to the stack of issues on which Mr. Bush just says "I didn't know, I didn't know, I didn't know …", and the media lets him get away with it. And the second defense is not acceptable because there is no way the Commander who allegedly granted the preferential treatment would admit to it, because he would simply be ruining his own reputation, and no one will do that. So we would expect Buck Staudt to say what he said. So we're still back to where we started, we don't know the exact truth because George W. Bush would not reveal the truth. It seems to me that the only way one can jump ahead of thousands of people on a waiting list is by getting some preferential treatment, there is no other explanation.

The second issue is whether George W. Bush was truthful when he said that he "fulfilled his duty". He sights the fact that he was honorably discharged as proof that he fulfilled his obligations. But this raises more questions than it answers. There are two unexplained gaps in Mr. Bush's service, and the fact that he got an honorable discharge seems to indicate that someone at the top may have taken care of his paperwork and ensured that he got that honorable discharge, even though he may not have fulfilled his Guard service. The first gap begins in May of 1972 when Mr. Bush left Texas and transferred to Alabama to work on the U.S. Senate campaign of Winston Blount, a family friend. He joined the Ready Reserve Unit in Montgomery, Alabama in September of that year. But according to published reports, the commander of that unit, the 187th, Lieutenant Colonel William Turnispeed, and the personnel officer, Kenneth K. Lott have repeatedly said they don't recall Mr. Bush showing up for duty in Alabama. The Associated Press investigated the issue and contacted a dozen members of the 187th, but no one recalls seeing Mr. Bush. To date, not a single individual has come forward and said that they served with Mr. Bush during this period. One man had stepped forward and said that he remembers serving with Bush, but the dates he gave did not jibe with the period in question and so his account has been discounted. It's just not credible for the President to claim that he served during that time and not a single person he allegedly served with would come forward and confirm that he or she remember him showing up for duty. Interestingly, there are some payroll records showing that Mr. Bush got paid for some of the time in question, but this only adds to the problem. Getting paid doesn't mean that he necessarily showed up for duty. So again, it appears that someone at the top was fixing his paperwork even though he may not have physically showed up for duty.

The second gap in Mr. Bush's service began on July 30, 1973 when he was granted permission to move to Boston so that he could attend Harvard Business School. Mr. Bush was supposed to report to another Reserve Force in order to complete his service. His spokespeople had claimed that he completed his National Guard service at a Boston area Air Force Reserve Unit, but there is no record of Bush ever reporting to a Boston-area unit. So you make the call on whether or not you think that Mr. Bush was truthful when he said "he fulfilled his duty". O'Reilly again allowed him to repeat this line without challenging it:

> *O'Reilly:* "They say you didn't register in Massachusetts. Is that bogus?"
> *Bush:* "I fulfilled my duties. I mean, this is—I did exactly what my commanders told me to do."
> *O'Reilly:* "OK. Do you think the swift boat vets' charges against Kerry are unfair?"

"Okay"? Is that all O'Reilly had to say? "Okay"? Mr. Bush said he fulfilled his duties without providing anything concrete and O'Reilly just says "Okay"? Come on O'Reilly, we know you can do better than that. Well, if Mr. Bush was a Democrat, that is. We know you don't want to embarrass Republicans.

As I said in the Author's Note at the beginning of this book, I am not a judgmental person. I believe that all of us have made mistakes, some small, some big, and I believe that we have the right to defend ourselves vigorously. **I WILL <u>NOT</u> MAKE JUDGEMENTS ABOUT PRESIDENT GEORGE W. BUSH'S HONESTY AND INTEGRITY**. I do not have all of the facts and would not claim to know what happened. The only reason why I raise the above two points about Mr. Bush is because O'Reilly has been one-sided in his quest for honesty and integrity from our politicians, and I wanted to show you that he is not the crusader he says he is, or the crusader people think he is. He is just out to get people he dislikes, and those who he likes are allowed to skate. This is not what being an Independent means.

7) Misrepresentation

You have to be very careful with O'Reilly when he presents what he calls the facts, especially when he utilizes statistics. He cleverly manipulates information and statistics, and bends them to support his arguments. For example, when President Bush was being criticized in the aftermath of hurricane Katrina for his policies towards the poor, O'Reilly sprung to his defense, and tried to use the U.S. poverty rate to prove that President Bush has done a better job on poverty than President Clinton. So here is how he presented the issue in his "Talking Points Memo" dated September 14, 2005 on *The O'Reilly Factor*:

> "... Halfway through President Clinton's tenure in office in 1996, the poverty rate was 13.7 percent. Halfway through President Bush's tenure, the rate is 12.7 percent, a full point lower...."

O'Reilly again repeated the same mantra on his September 19th edition of *The O'Reilly Factor* with Dick Morris:

> "... And the poverty rate stood at 13.7 percent halfway through Clinton's tenure. It is 12.7 percent halfway through Bush's two terms."

Now, on the face of it, these statements would give you the impression that Mr. Bush has done a better job than Mr. Clinton on poverty in the United States. And this is why I think that O'Reilly is a genius at spin and deception. The above statements are factually correct. The figures, as he quoted them, are true. But the big whopper is that the figures don't prove what O'Reilly wants them to prove, namely that Mr. Bush has done a better job on poverty than Mr. Clinton, because when you look at the poverty rate over time you will see that the poverty rate came *down* every single year under Mr. Clinton whereas it went *up* every single year under Mr. Bush:

U.S. Poverty Rate

1993	1994	1995	1996	1997	1998	1999	2000	2001	2002	2003	2004
15.1	14.5	13.8	13.7	13.3	12.7	11.9	11.3	11.7	12.1	12.5	12.7

Source: U.S. Census Bureau

As the table above shows, Mr. Clinton started in 1993 with a poverty rate of 15.1%, and the rate came down every single year to the point where it was 11.3% when he left office, nearly a 4 percentage point drop during his tenure. Mr. Bush took over at 11.3% and the poverty rate went *up* each and every year to the point where it was 12.7% in 2004, 1.4% *higher* than when he took office in 2001. So the poverty rate has gotten *worse* year after year under the Bush Administration, not better, and Bush is not doing a good job on poverty as O'Reilly wanted his audience to believe. That's the fact. Congressman Charlie Rangel busted O'Reilly when he tried to spin the statistics again on his September 27th edition of *The O'Reilly Factor*. Confronted by the fact that more Americans fell into poverty under Bush, O'Reilly then quickly and deftly changed tactics and blamed 9/11 for the increased poverty rate:

> *O'Reilly*: "Lower poverty rate halfway through Bush's term than Clinton, that's the fact."
> *Rangel*: "It's a sharp increase than before …"
> *O'Reilly*: "Because of the 9/11 attacks. All right, Congressman."
> *Rangel*: "It's not so, 9/11 had nothing to do with poverty."
> *O'Reilly*: "Yes, it did. It sent us into a recession and the lower level service jobs fled, and you know it because it happened right here in New York, where you're the congressman."

I guess that's the last we will hear from O'Reilly on poverty rate and the Bush Administration. I have no problem if O'Reilly wants to argue that 9/11 caused the poverty rate to increase under the Bush Administration, but that's not what he started out arguing. He tried to present the case that the Bush Administration was doing a better job than the Clinton Administration on poverty, which is absolutely false however you look at it.

Another area of egregious misrepresentation by O'Reilly occurred in 2001 after President Clinton left office and George W. Bush took over as president. O'Reilly tried to make the case over and over again that Mr. Clinton handed Mr. Bush a bad economy:

"Then the economy fell apart just in time to greet Mr. Bush."[11]

"In Mr. Clinton's last year, the economy was heading south anyway."[12]

"The economic recession began in Mr. Clinton's last year in office and has been exacerbated by the war on terror and Iraq. To be fair, after the stock market bubble of the '90's, no president could have avoided an economic pull back. But it is a fact that, overall, Mr. Clinton handed one big mess to Mr. Bush."[13]

Of all the dishonest claims that O'Reilly has made against Mr. Clinton, this is probably the most unfounded. Mr. Clinton did not hand Mr. Bush "one big mess" as O'Reilly claimed. O'Reilly is dealing in propaganda, not facts. I will get into the facts in a moment, but first I just want to speculate on why O'Reilly took this line of attack against Mr. Clinton. I can think of two reasons. Firstly, I think he wanted to put a dampener on Mr. Clinton's excellent and envious economic record. Secondly, he wanted to lay the foundation for an excuse for Mr. Bush's just in case the economy had gone into a recession. The latter was sort of an insurance policy to protect Mr. Bush from criticism and avoid holding him accountable had things gone wrong. A clever tactic from O'Reilly, isn't it? Now you know why O'Reilly gets paid the big bucks, right? But of course the economy did not crumble as O'Reilly predicted, which adds another stroke against his dismal record of prediction making. Anyway, getting back to the main point, an examination of the facts and statistics contradict O'Reilly's claim that the economy was falling apart in 2000. There never was any economic mess in 2000 as O'Reilly lamented. Let's take a look at two of the key economic indicators of the economy—Unemployment and Economic Growth—and you will see what I mean:

i) Unemployment

The unemployment rate when Mr. Clinton left office was 4 percent. This is actually the lowest in the eight years of Mr. Clinton's reign, so the unemployment rate was actually trending downwards. Below is a table showing the unemployment rate during Mr. Clinton's eight years in office:

U.S. Unemployment Rate

1993	1994	1995	1996	1997	1998	1999	2000
6.9%	6.1%	5.6%	5.4%	4.9%	4.5%	4.2%	4.0%

Source: Bureau of Labor Statistics

As you can see, it's really a perfect record for Mr. Clinton. Unemployment declined steadily over his presidency, from 6.9% in 1993 to an enviable 4% in

2000. So what is O'Reilly talking about when he says that Mr. Clinton handed Mr. Bush one big mess? Clearly, O'Reilly is dealing in propaganda, not facts. There is no basis whatsoever for his claim that the economy was heading south when Mr. Clinton left office. Unemployment is one of the major indicators of a country's economic health. I would argue that it is *the* major indicator, and if unemployment is at 4%, you have to be a lunatic to argue that the economy is in a mess.

To put Mr. Clinton's record in some context, let's compare Mr. Clinton's unemployment figures with Mr. Reagan's unemployment figures. When Mr. Reagan left office in 1988 the unemployment rate was 5.5%. The lowest unemployment rate ever achieved by Mr. Reagan was 5.5%. Below are the statistics for the Reagan years:

<u>U.S. Unemployment Rate</u>

1981	1982	1983	1984	1985	1986	1987	1988
7.6%	9.7%	9.6%	7.5%	7.2%	7.0%	6.2%	5.5%

Source: Bureau of Labor Statistics

The average unemployment rate over Mr. Clinton's eight years was 5.2%; while the average unemployment rate over Mr. Reagan's eight years was 7.5%. Clearly, however you look at it, unemployment during the Reagan years was worse than the Clinton years. Mr. Clinton passed on a relatively healthy economy to Mr. Bush, contrary to the lies put out by Bill O'Reilly and some others in the right-wing media. It is interesting that these people did not complain when Mr. Reagan left an economy with a 5.5% unemployment rate to George H. W. Bush. Instead, they heaped praise upon Mr. Reagan for his handling of the economy. But in the case of Mr. Clinton, O'Reilly somehow tried to argue that the 4% unemployment rate at the end of Mr. Clinton's reign was "one big mess". This clearly shows you how partisan and intellectually dishonest this guy is.

ii) Economic Growth

GDP (Gross Domestic Product) growth in 2000 was 3.7 percent. Compared to previous years under President Clinton, this does not in any way represent a dramatic deviation from the average growth rate over his eight years. The GDP growth rates during Mr. Clinton's tenure are as follows:

U.S. Economic Growth

1993	1994	1995	1996	1997	1998	1999	2000
2.7%	4.0%	2.5%	3.7%	4.5%	4.2%	4.5%	3.7%

Source: U.S. Census Bureau

The average growth rate over Mr. Clinton's eight years is 3.7 percent, so the growth rate in 2000 does not in any way represent a decline. The fact that the growth rate fell in 2000 by 0.8 percent compared to 1999 does not mean that the economy was heading into a recession. It is typical for growth to fluctuate from year to year. Take the Reagan years for example:

U.S. Economic Growth

1981	1982	1983	1984	1985	1986	1987	1988
2.5%	-1.9%	4.5%	7.2%	4.1%	3.5%	3.4%	4.1%

Source: U.S. Census Bureau

As you can see, under Mr. Reagan, growth declined in 1982 but picked up in 1983 and 1984, only to decline again in 1985, 1986 & 1987, but finally crept up again in 1988. When Mr. Clinton left office in 2000 the growth rate was 3.7 percent, only 0.4 percent lower than when Mr. Reagan left office, but well within the average achieved by Mr. Clinton over his eight years. In fact Mr. Clinton achieved a higher average growth rate over his eight years than Mr. Reagan—3.7 percent for Mr. Clinton versus 3.4 percent for Mr. Reagan. It's astonishing that O'Reilly and the right-wing media constantly applaud Mr. Reagan for his economic legacy but does the opposite to Mr. Clinton who has a similar if not better record. Hypocrisy is the word.

8) Dramatization

No discussion of Bill O'Reilly and his techniques can be complete without talking about the use of drama. Where would O'Reilly be without Dramatization? He knows how to inject drama and instill emotions into certain issues to move the audience in the direction he wants them to go. He picks the particular issues and battles he wants to fight and then delivers an almost flawless performance to impress and convince his audience. One has to give him credit. I may sound a bit cynical here, so don't get me wrong. I'm not saying that dramatization per se is bad, but to use drama to peddle right-wing propaganda and make political arguments is just plain ridiculous. When dealing with Democrats, for instance, O'Reilly would inject more emotion into the presentation, much more so than when dealing with Republicans. He is not afraid to show his anger and disgust when reporting on Democrats who he believes are corrupt or incompetent. But there are corrupt and incompetent Republicans too, aren't they? But you don't see O'Reilly injecting the same degree of emotion when reporting on them. So he clearly dramatizes with a purpose, the net effect of which is to turn his audience against Democrats and make Republicans look more favorable. Maybe this is a subconscious manifestation of his bias, but it also points to his intentions. O'Reilly did not show nearly the same emotion when dealing with the GOP scandals (DeLay, Abramoff, & Cunningham) as when he dealt with so-called scandals in the Clinton era (even though no one higher up in the Clinton Administration was ever indicted or charged with any illegality). He did not show the same contempt for corruption in 2005/2006 as he did back in the late 1990's. And one cannot argue that he is getting old or tired, because he is as feisty as ever now or even feistier on other issues. So one can only conclude that the difference in emotion and drama that he injects is a deliberate act on his part to influence his audience accordingly. His end game is to portray Democrats as corrupt and incompetent, while at the same time defend and sanitize Republicans when similar allegations against them arise.

I'm always fascinated by the way he presents his Talking Points Memo each night on his show *The O'Reilly Factor*. Nine times out of ten, his talking points memo is an anti-Democratic, anti-Liberal rant that is perfectly choreographed and packaged to convince his viewers that he is presenting facts. If someone who doesn't know who Bill O'Reilly is should watch and listen to these talking points memo, he or she will probably end up believing most if not all of what he says, because he looks convincing, he looks sincere, and he comes over as being very confident about what he is saying. But the fact is that nine times out of ten his talking points memo is either factually incorrect or rife with bias and propaganda, or both. Look out for my dissection of some of his talking points memo, and you will see for yourself how partisan and inaccurate they often are.

So this is the framework within which I would argue that O'Reilly operates. Based on my assessment of his work, he is an agenda driven journalist, and I am presenting additional facts to back up my thesis in the remaining Chapters. O'Reilly comes to each issue from an ideological perspective and is not interested in objectivity and fairness. He puts on a good show, claiming to be fair and bal-anced, and non-political, but the reality is that he is not. There is no doubt in my mind that he favors Republicans and Conservatives. So whenever you listen to O'Reilly again or read his writings, look out for these propaganda devices, and you will be able to easily debunk many, if not, all of his fallacious and arguments:

Omission

Selectivity

Fabrication

Demonization/Repetition/Association/Diversion

Oversimplification

Double Standard

Misrepresentation

Dramatization

APPENDIX 1A

Text of Clinton's Op-Ed Piece as it Appeared in *The New York Times*, Feb. 18, 2001.

My Reasons for the Pardons

By William Jefferson Clinton

CHAPPAQUA, N.Y., Feb. 18—Because of the intense scrutiny and criticism of the pardons of Marc Rich and his partner Pincus Green and because legitimate concerns have been raised, I want to explain what I did and why.

First, I want to make some general comments about pardons and commutations of sentences. Article II of the Constitution gives the president broad and unreviewable power to grant "Reprieves and Pardons" for all offenses against the United States. The Supreme Court has ruled that the pardon power is granted "[t]o the [president] ..., and it is granted without limit" (United States v. Klein). Justice Oliver Wendell Holmes declared that "[a] pardon ... is ... the determination of the ultimate authority that the public welfare will be better served by [the pardon] ..." (Biddle v. Perovich). A president may conclude a pardon or commutation is warranted for several reasons: the desire to restore full citizenship rights, including voting, to people who have served their sentences and lived within the law since; a belief that a sentence was excessive or unjust; personal circumstances that warrant compassion; or other unique circumstances.

The exercise of executive clemency is inherently controversial. The reason the framers of our Constitution vested this broad power in the Executive Branch was to assure that the president would have the freedom to do what he deemed to be the right thing, regardless of how unpopular a decision might be. Some of the uses of the power have been extremely controversial, such as President Washington's pardons of leaders of the Whiskey Rebellion, President Harding's commutation of the sentence of Eugene Debs, President Nixon's commutation of the sentence of James Hoffa, President Ford's pardon of former President Nixon, President Carter's pardon of Vietnam War draft resisters, and President Bush's 1992 pardon of six Iran-contra defendants, including former Defense Secretary Weinberger, which assured the end of that investigation.

On Jan. 20, 2001, I granted 140 pardons and issued 36 commutations. During my presidency, I issued a total of approximately 450 pardons and commutations, compared to 406 issued by President Reagan during his two terms. During his four years, President Carter issued 566 pardons and commutations, while in the same length of time President Bush granted 77. President Ford issued 409 during the slightly more than two years he was president.

The vast majority of my Jan. 20 pardons and reprieves went to people who are not well known. Some had been sentenced pursuant to mandatory-sentencing drug laws, and I felt that they had served long enough, given the particular circumstances of the individual cases. Many of these were first-time nonviolent offenders with no previous criminal records; in some cases, codefendants had received significantly shorter sentences. At the attorney general's request, I commuted one death sentence because the defendant's principal accuser later changed his testimony, casting doubt on the defendant's guilt. In some cases, I granted pardons because I felt the individuals had been unfairly treated and punished pursuant to the Independent Counsel statute then in existence. The remainder of the pardons and commutations were granted for a wide variety of fact-based reasons, but the common denominator was that the cases, like that of Patricia Hearst, seemed to me deserving of executive clemency. Overwhelmingly, the pardons went to people who had been convicted and served their time, so the impact of the pardon was principally to restore the person's civil rights. Many of these, including some of the more controversial, had vigorous bipartisan support.

The pardons that have attracted the most criticism have been the pardons of Marc Rich and Pincus Green, who were indicted in 1983 on charges of racketeering and mail and wire fraud, arising out of their oil business.

Ordinarily, I would have denied pardons in this case simply because these men did not return to the United States to face the charges against them. However, I decided to grant the pardons in this unusual case for the following legal and foreign policy reasons: (1) I understood that the other oil companies that had structured transactions like those on which Mr. Rich and Mr. Green were indicted were instead sued civilly by the government; (2) I was informed that, in 1985, in a related case against a trading partner of Mr. Rich and Mr. Green, the Energy Department, which was responsible for enforcing the governing law, found that the manner in which the Rich/Green companies had accounted for these transactions was proper; (3) two highly regarded tax experts, Bernard Wolfman of Harvard Law School and Martin Ginsburg of Georgetown University Law Center, reviewed the transactions in question and concluded that the companies "were correct in their U.S. income tax treatment of all the items in question, and [that] there was no unreported federal income or additional tax liability attributable to any of the [challenged] transactions"; (4) in order to settle the government's case against them, the two men's companies had paid approximately $200 million in fines, penalties and taxes, most of which might not even have been warranted under the Wolfman/Ginsburg analysis that the companies had followed the law and correctly reported their income; (5) the Justice Department in 1989 rejected the use of racketeering statutes in tax cases like this one, a position that The Wall Street Journal editorial page, among others, agreed with at the time; (6) it was my understanding that Deputy Attorney General Eric Holder's position on the pardon application was "neutral, leaning for"; (7) the case for the pardons was reviewed and advocated not only by my former White House counsel Jack Quinn but also by three distinguished Republican attorneys: Leonard Garment, a former Nixon White House official; William Bradford Reynolds, a former high-ranking official in the Reagan Justice Department; and Lewis Libby, now Vice President Cheney's chief of staff; (8) finally, and importantly, many present and former high-ranking Israeli officials of both major political parties and leaders of Jewish communities in America and Europe urged the pardon of Mr. Rich because of his contributions and services to Israeli charitable causes, to the Mossad's efforts to rescue and evacuate Jews from hostile countries, and to the peace process through sponsorship of education and health programs in Gaza and the West Bank.

While I was troubled by the criminalization of the charges against Mr. Rich and Mr. Green, I also wanted to assure the government's ability to pursue any Energy Department, civil tax or other charges that might be available and warranted. I knew the men's companies had settled their disputes with the government, but I did not know what personal liability the individuals might still have for Energy Department or other violations.

Therefore, I required them to waive any and all defenses, including their statute of limitations defenses, to any civil charge the government might bring against them. Before I granted the pardons, I received from their lawyer a letter confirming that they "waive any and all defenses which could be raised to the lawful imposition of civil fines or penalties in connection with the actions and transactions alleged in the indictment against them pending in the Southern District of New York."

I believe my pardon decision was in the best interests of justice. If the two men were wrongly indicted in the first place, justice has been done. On the other hand, if they do personally owe money for Energy Department penalties, unpaid taxes or civil fines, they can now be sued civilly, as others in their position apparently were, a result that might not have been possible without the waiver, because civil statutes of limitations may have run while they were out of the United States.

While I was aware of and took into account the fact that the United States attorney for the Southern District of New York did not support these pardons, in retrospect, the process would have been better served had I sought her views directly. Further, I regret that Mr. Holder did not have more time to review the case. However, I believed the essential facts were before me, and I felt the foreign policy considerations and the legal arguments justified moving forward.

The suggestion that I granted the pardons because Mr. Rich's former wife, Denise, made political contributions and contributed to the Clinton library foundation is utterly false. There was absolutely no quid pro quo. Indeed, other friends and financial supporters sought pardons in cases which, after careful consideration based on the information available to me, I determined I could not grant.

In the last few months of my term, many, many people called, wrote or came up to me asking that I grant or at least consider granting clemency in various cases. These people included friends, family members, former spouses of applicants, supporters, acquaintances, Republican and Democratic members of Congress, journalists and total strangers. I believe that the president can and should listen to such requests, although they cannot determine his decision on the merits. There is only one prohibition: there can be no quid pro quo. And there certainly was not in this or any of the other pardons and commutations I granted.

I am accustomed to the rough and tumble of politics, but the accusations made against me in this case have been particularly painful because for eight years I worked hard to make good decisions for the American people. I want every American to know that, while you may disagree with this decision, I made it on the merits as I saw them, and I take full responsibility for it.

Footnotes to Chapter One:

1) Who's Looking Out for You, Bill O'Reilly, Page 53.

2) The Autobiography Of An Individualist, Frank Chodorov.

3) Who's Looking Out for You, Bill O'Reilly, Page 65.

4) Who's Looking Out for You, Bill O'Reilly, Page 67.

5) The O'Reilly Factor, December 12, 2005.

6) Who's Looking Out for You, Bill O'Reilly, Page 54.

7) The O'Reilly Factor, October 17, 2006.

8) Who's Looking Out for You, Bill O'Reilly, Page 61.

9) Who's Looking Out for You, Bill O'Reilly, Page 52.

10) Plan Of Attack, Bob Woodward, Pages 249—250.

11) Who's Looking Out for You, Bill O'Reilly, Page 53.

12) Who's Looking Out for You, Bill O'Reilly, Page 55.

13) Who's Looking Out for You, Bill O'Reilly, Page 61.

2

"I Am An Independent"

Bill O'Reilly constantly asserts that he is an "Independent", but what exactly does that mean? Yes it's true that he switched from being a *registered* Republican to a *registered* Independent a few years ago, according to published reports, and right now he is a registered Independent on *paper*, but does that mean that he is a *true* Independent when it comes to dealing with Republican versus Democrat? Does he apply the *same* level of scrutiny to both Republicans and Democrats? Does he favor one over the other in his political commentary? Is he someone who is difficult to figure out in terms of what his political beliefs are? The answers to all of these questions are really quite simple for anyone who watches *The O'Reilly Factor* regularly or have read the writings of Bill O'Reilly: The fact is that he is not an Independent in the real sense of the word; he is a partisan political hack, not much different from say Rush Limbaugh or Sean Hannity. A truly independent person is someone whose political views are somewhat hard to figure out, someone who does not come down along predictable ideological lines, and someone whom you cannot guess easily who they might have voted for, or who they will vote for. People like Tim Russert, Peter Jennings, Jim Lehrer, Barbara Walters, and others like them, come to mind as being truly independent journalists. When you watch and listen to these people you cannot come away with a notion of whom they support politically. With O'Reilly, it's almost always obvious who he has voted for or who he will vote for. Is there anyone who honestly believes that Bill O'Reilly will vote for a Democrat?

O'Reilly never misses an opportunity to bludgeon Democrats, but often goes to lengths to defend Republicans. Have you counted how many times O'Reilly has rushed to the defense of President George W. Bush, for example? I've lost count. Democrats are scrutinized in the most cynical manner, while Republicans are often let off the hook with little or no critical analysis. O'Reilly is also always quick to pronounce judgment on Democrats, but when it comes to Republicans, he holds his fire and says he doesn't have all the facts and cannot jump to conclusions. But he has tried and convicted Democrats Bill Clinton, Hillary Clinton, Al Gore, and Jessie Jackson in the media, just to name a few, even though none of these people have ever been convicted of any wrongdoing in a court of law. On the other hand, Republicans who were accused of moral and ethical lapses are never vilified in such a way. O'Reilly doesn't show the same contempt towards Tom DeLay, for example.

Bill Clinton's legacy

In a May 11, 2001 article in WorldNetDaily.com, here is how Bill O'Reilly summed up the legacy of Bill Clinton:

> "There are times when I feel guilty for hammering Bill Clinton.
> He is a man who accomplished a miracle, rising up from humble beginnings in Hope, Ark., to become the most powerful person in the world. And he did it with little help. Mr. Clinton was raised primarily by his flamboyant mother, and although she adored him, she could offer him little in the way of worldly influence. I admire self-made people and William Jefferson Clinton is all that. But that is where my admiration stops.
> We are all suffering right now because of Bill Clinton's presidency, and it has nothing to do with his moral failings. It has everything to do with his *policy* failings.
> The current earnings recession and economic slowdown has its roots in Mr. Clinton's final year in office. During that time, he turned away from managing the economy and devoted a huge amount of time fund-raising for himself (the Clinton Library), his wife's senatorial campaign and the Democratic Party.
> Spurned by Al Gore, Mr. Clinton traveled not to deliver a political message, but to grab your wallet. His wanderings turned into a giant mobile flea market where he sold his time and presence for major dollars.
> Mr. Clinton also became obsessed with brokering a peace agreement between the Israelis and the Palestinians. This, of course, led to nothing but more hatred and violence, as we are seeing now on a daily basis.
> With the president's attention diverted, Alan Greenspan and his merry band inexplicably kept the U.S. money supply tight, even as manufacturing orders, especially in high-tech, were slowing drastically. There was no political pressure on the Fed to cut rates as Mr. Clinton was paying scant attention. Thus, in December, when Greenspan still declined to cut interest rates, the economic dam broke and the waters of declining earnings flooded the stock market.
> The bad economic news was compounded by the fact that Mr. Clinton never had an energy policy and allowed the OPEC nations to cut oil production without challenge. Energy prices soared, cutting into corporate profits and

gutting the take-home pay of American workers. Mr. Clinton knew there weren't enough oil refineries in the USA but made no attempt to build any. He also knew that America's dependence on foreign oil was at an all-time high but failed to encourage consumers to conserve energy, because that might annoy his SUV-driving soccer mom base.

Bill Clinton fiddled while oil and natural gas burned. And finally, the nation's most powerful state, California, simply ran out of power.

In his last days as president, Mr. Clinton signed a number of environmental orders but never once warned anybody about the growing scarcity of energy. To say he was pandering to the greens is a gross understatement.

Bill Clinton's education policies have also been a disaster. Despite a massive amount of federal spending, 60 percent of the nation's poor fourth-graders still can barely read. Mr. Clinton was a champion of educational spending but made no attempt to tie the money to performance. This endeared him to the teachers' unions but didn't do much for at-risk kids who desperately need discipline and learning standards.

The second most at-risk group in America are poor seniors. And what did Mr. Clinton do for them? Drug prices are the highest they've ever been. Some seniors are still traveling to Mexico and Canada to get their prescriptions filled.

But prices for illegal drugs are the lowest they've ever been. Street heroin and cocaine are readily available all over the USA with no waiting. That's because narcotics continue to flood into this country while Bill Clinton and his drug czar, Gen. Barry McCaffrey, introduced absolutely no effective federal measures designed to cut either supply or demand. Mr. Clinton's NAFTA agreement with Mexico allowed for freer passage through our southern border. The "traffic" that ensued had little do with cars and trucks.

So there's your Clinton legacy, and you can take it over to Barbra Streisand's house and drop it on her lawn. The president wasted one full year lying about his sexcapades and another year asking people for money. The other six years he talked a really good game.

But talk is cheap and gas is not. If our cars and homes and stores ran on hot air, Bill Clinton might be right up there with Abe Lincoln."

Obviously, the objective of O'Reilly's column is to try to destroy Mr. Clinton's reputation and belittle his accomplishments. O'Reilly wasn't interested in the being fair and balanced. What he did was to pick out all of the bad stuff and blame Mr. Clinton for them. But not only that, he *exaggerated* the bad stuff and acted like these things never existed before, and were *created* by the Clinton Administration. And most importantly, O'Reilly left out all, yes all, of the accomplishments of the Clinton Administration. He didn't mention one single positive thing about the Clinton Administration. This article by itself is an indictment of the so-called independence of Bill O'Reilly. Let's take his arguments one by one.

First, he blames Mr. Clinton for the economic slowdown that was occurring under President George W. Bush. If O'Reilly knew anything about Economics, he should know that growth and prosperity comes in cycles. After eight years of economic expansion under President Clinton's leadership, the economy is bound to slow down a little. In fact, never before in the history of America has there been an economic expansion that lasted so long. Instead of giving credit to Mr. Clinton, O'Reilly blasts Mr. Clinton for not ensuring that the economic expansion goes on and on. One of the reasons why I think the economy slowed down was uncertainty regarding the Bush Administration's policies. People didn't have the same confidence in George W. Bush and they had in Bill Clinton. Confidence is what drives the economy. When people are optimistic about the future they invest more, they spend more, they take more risks, etc. etc., and this leads to economic expansion. That's the bottom line.

O'Reilly says "there was no political pressure on the Fed to cut rates as Mr. Clinton was paying scant attention", but this shows O'Reilly's fundamental misunderstanding of how the Federal Reserve operates. No one, including Mr. Clinton, would have been able to put pressure on Alan Greenspan to cut interest rates. The Federal Reserve is independent of the government, that's the way the system was designed. Furthermore, Alan Greenspan is not the only person who makes the decision whether or not to change interest rate, it is a Board that votes, and Mr. Greenspan is just one member of the Board, albeit he is the Chairman. So this focus on Alan Greenspan was just political posturing from O'Reilly, and it demonstrates his ignorance of economic issues.

Next, he blames Mr. Clinton for the fighting in the Middle East that was occurring at that time, which really wasn't all that terrible compared to other periods. He claims that Mr. Clinton's efforts to try to bring about peace between the Israelis and the Palestinians led to more violence. How absurd is that? O'Reilly doesn't explain how he arrived at that conclusion; he just makes an assertion. But his assertion is fallacious, because there has always been violence in that part of the world, and the violence during the period in question had nothing to do with the peace negotiations. The violence goes up and down depending on the internal situation in that region. This guy's hatred for Mr. Clinton is so deep that it's getting in the way of whatever commonsense he has left.

Then he blames Mr. Clinton for the California energy situation, blasts Mr. Clinton for failing to improve the grades of America's Fourth-Graders, and holds Mr. Clinton accountable for the falling price of illegal drugs, of all things.

Remember the notion of *Oversimplification* I touch on in Chapter One? It is very much in play here. Anyone can blame anyone for anything, but the key question is whether or not it is valid to do so. It is valid to blame Mr. Clinton solely for the educational failures in the United States? Can we blame President Reagan and President Bush Sr. for the failures prior to that? Can we blame President George W. Bush for the current failures? This is no way to engage in serious analysis, and O'Reilly ought to know better. Regarding the energy situation, should we blame George W. Bush for the three-dollar a gallon gas price that we just went through, or for our failure to become more energy independent as a nation? This is junk journalism at it's worse, and it's the exact sort of thing that drove me to write this book.

Douglas Wead, Linda Tripp, Dick Morris

On February 21, 2005, in his "Personal Story Segment" on *The O'Reilly Factor*, O'Reilly decries the secret taping of George W. Bush by a friend of his, a guy by the name of Douglas Wead, who ended up writing a book unfavorable to Mr. Bush. Here are O'Reilly's opening remarks:

> "Tonight, there's a new book out written by a close friend of the Bush Family, at least he used to be. The guy's name is Douglas Wead, whose last name is appropriate.
> Apparently, Wead secretly taped George W. Bush in 1998 when he was thinking about running for the presidency. Wead then used those tapes to sell a book to Simon and Shuster, which is owned by Viacom and the parent company of CBS.
> Wead does not quote from the secret tapes, but has used them to promote his book, playing the tapes for 'The New York Times', among others.
> This is just sleazy, but is acceptable, it seems, to Simon and Shuster. Joining us now from New York is Dennis Kneale, the managing editor of 'Forbes' magazine.
> Now I'm not going to mention the name of the book. I don't want anybody to buy it. I don't care what the book says particularly. But I think the fact that now in America you can secretly tape anybody and then use this to make money is—sends a chilling message and it's disgraceful. How do you see it?"

O'Reilly was fuming that his pal, George W. Bush (a Republican) was secretly taped. He says now that he thinks it's disgraceful to secretly tape someone and use it to promote your own agenda and gain publicity. But I don't recall O'Reilly being the slightest upset when Linda Trip secretly taped Monica Lewinsky back in 1997. He didn't rush to the defense of Monica Lewinsky or Bill Clinton the same way he rushed to defend George W. Bush. He didn't condemn Linda Trip the same way he condemned Douglas Wead. I guess he didn't see a problem with secretly taping someone back then and using it to promote one's own agenda, as Linda Trip did, obviously because it got Bill Clinton (a Democrat) into trouble and started the whole impeachment trial. O'Reilly's standards have surely *evolved* over time. But I wouldn't be surprised if he changes his standard again should, say, Hillary Clinton (a Democrat) be secretly taped by someone. Do you think he will come to Hillary Clinton's defense? I would bet that he might flip once again and find a rationale to justify the secret taping of a Democrat.

O'Reilly is a close friend of Dick Morris, the former Clinton adviser, and Dick Morris is an analyst on O'Reilly's show *The O'Reilly Factor* on a fairly regular basis. O'Reilly does not have a problem with Dick Morris talking about the most confidential conversations he has had with the Clintons when he was working for them. In fact, O'Reilly never misses an opportunity to nudge Dick Morris into divulging those conversations on his show. As most of you may know, Dick Morris subsequently made a lot of money writing about the Clintons after he resigned. Three of his best selling books are about the Clintons: *Because He Could, Rewriting History, and Condi versus Hillary*. O'Reilly's moral relativism is startling, isn't it? He has a problem with people close to George Bush betraying George W. Bush, but then turns around and teams up with Dick Morris to betray the Clintons. Where is O'Reilly's standard of decency? If he is so much concerned about people's privacy across the board, he would not have someone like Dick Morris on his show revealing confidential conversations and dealings he has had with the Clintons. Do you think O'Reilly will one day have a former adviser to a Republican President talk so candidly about his or her former boss? Don't hold your breath.

George Soros, Richard Mellon Schaife, Rupert Murdoch

Many people who follow O'Reilly may certainly have heard of George Soros, because O'Reilly has done so many segments on him and has lambasted him mercilessly for his legitimate involvement in our political process. But they may not have heard of Richard Mellon Scaife, because O'Reilly (and the Fox News Channel) have largely ignored Mr. Scaife's involvement in the political process. According to a Washington Post article of May 3, 1999, Richard Mellon Scaife has been one of the most generous donors to Conservative causes in American history. He has given away more than $600 million, of which about $340 million went to funding a "war of ideas" against American liberalism. In the 1990's he reportedly gave $2.3 million to the American Spectator magazine to dig up dirt on then President Clinton, and supported other Conservative groups that harassed Mr. Clinton and his administration. O'Reilly has been virtually silent on Scaife. He clearly does not see a problem with Scaife pouring millions of dollars into the fight against Liberalism. He also has never demonized Scaife the way he demonized George Soros, because he most likely welcomes Scaife's anti-Liberal funding.

One of the things O'Reilly has done on a regular basis is to bring guests on his show who have dug up dirt on George Soros, so that they could tell his viewers what they found out. O'Reilly himself told his viewers that George Soros didn't care about his (Soros') dyeing father, obviously trying to make Soros appear inhumane. O'Reilly also made it known to his viewers that George Soros was indicted in *France* for insider trading. Now, we all know that O'Reilly has no respect for France, as demonstrated by his numerous inflammatory anti-French statements, but in this instance he is willing to sight the French judicial system as the standard for judging George Soros. It is true that George Soros was fined 2.2 million Euros for buying and selling Societe Generale shares in 1988 in France, but other than that George Soros has had a clean record. He was never indicted or convicted in the *United States* for anything. O'Reilly wanted to give everyone the impression that George Soros is a criminal, and so he used the French judicial system as the standard. This is the same France of which O'Reilly says "When are we Americans going to wise up? How many times does the French government led by Jacques Chirac, Have to put us all in danger before we get the picture? France is helping worldwide terrorism."[1]

O'Reilly also seems to forget that his boss, Rupert Murdoch, is a wealthy man who makes a lot of money promoting right-wing ideology. Nearly all of the major media entities owned by Rupert Murdoch are right-wing media outlets—The Fox News Channel, which O'Reilly works for, the New York Post, and the Mirror newspaper in England, just to name a few. I have no problem with Mr. Murdoch doing what he is doing. It's a free country and that is his right, just like it is Mr. Soros's right to fund whatever causes he believes in. While O'Reilly may argue that Mr. Murdoch is engaged in it as a "business", I don't think that it makes one bit of difference, because I am sure Mr. Murdoch is aware that people are influenced by whatever his media outlets put out, much more so than by what Mr. Soros's entities put out. So business or not, the effect is the same: people are influenced one way or the other and a political objective is achieved. Hence, O'Reilly's lop-sided focus only on the money people on the Left is once again proof that he is not an independent analyst as he claims.

Tom DeLay, Nancy Peloci, Gary Condit

Bill O'Reilly constantly insults Nancy Peloci, the former Democratic Minority Leader of the House of Representative and now Speaker of the House of Representative, simply because she is a Liberal. I mentioned one such insult in Chapter One where he called her a "nut" and a "fanatic". Nancy Peloci at that time was the equivalent of Tom DeLay on the Republican side, and unlike Tom DeLay, she was never accused of any wrongdoing and she has no investigation pending against her. Yet, incredibly, O'Reilly talks about her as if she is an outlaw. But on Tom DeLay, one of the most morally challenged politicians of our times, O'Reilly has been virtually silent, and has refrained from condemning DeLay and calling for his resignation. As I promised, here is a list of the misdeeds and alleged misdeeds of Tom DeLay:

1) Mr. DeLay was admonished *three times* by the House of Representatives for unethical conduct. These are not just allegations; these are finding by the House of Representatives, and Tom DeLay has been formally reprimanded by the House for the following:

> (i) Tom DeLay offered to endorse the son of a Republican congressman if that congressman (Nick Smith) voted "yes" on the Medicare prescription-drug bill.
> (ii) Tom DeLay held a golf fundraiser with energy companies days before legislation affecting these companies came up on the floor of the Congress for voting.
> (iii) Tom DeLay used government resources (the FAA) to track the plane of a group of Democratic politicians leaving Texas protesting the redistricting legislation in the Texas State Legislature.

2) Mr. DeLay allegedly funneled about half of a million dollars from his campaign coffers to his wife and daughter as "salaries" for work done on his campaign. Now, it is not uncommon for politicians to hire their family or relatives and pay them out of campaign funds, but half of a million dollars? This stinks. Actions like these should be against the law in my opinion, because it is clearly an abuse of power. But where was Bill O'Reilly? What was Bill O'Reilly's opinion on the matter? We simply don't know, because Bill O'Reilly refused to pass judgment on Tom DeLay. Do you think Bill O'Reilly would have been so silent had this been a Democrat?

3) Mr. DeLay made 3 trips abroad, all allegedly funded by illegal means:

(i) In 1997 DeLay made a trip to Moscow ostensibly paid for by the National Center for Public Policy Research, but investigations done by the Washington Post newspaper revealed that the trip may have actually been paid for by a mysterious company registered in the Bahamas connected with lobbying in support of the Russian government.

(ii) In 2000 Tom DeLay made a golfing trip to Scotland. According to the Washington Post newspaper DeLay's air fare was charged to an American Express credit card issued to Jack Abramoff, a registered Washington lobbyist at the time, who has since been convicted and sentenced to jail for illegal activities unrelated to Tom DeLay. Lobbyists are generally barred from paying for lawmakers' travel, even if the expenses are reimbursed by an authorized source. During this same trip, other expenses were billed to a credit card used by Edwin A. Buckham, another registered lobbyist. Under House rules, lawmakers may not accept anything of value, including entertainment, recreation, or meals, from anyone if the value of the gift exceeds $50.00.

(iii) DeLay made a trip to South Korea in 2001 that was paid for by the Korea-US Exchange Council, a business-financed entity that registered as a foreign agent—essentially a lobbyist for a foreign country.

Add to this lengthy "rap sheet" the fact that three of DeLay's political aides were indicted on money laundering charges involving efforts to steer corporate contributions into Texas state races, and federal prosecutors and congressional committees were forced to investigate the activities of two of his allies, Michael Scanlon, and Jack Abramoff (mentioned above). But where was Mr. Ethics—Bill O'Reilly? For a man who claims to be looking out for the folks, he's been awfully silent on the corrupt Tom DeLay. I suspect if this were a Democrat, Bill O'Reilly would be foaming at the mouth, and would have launched into a daily crusade against him the way he did against Democrat Gary Condit. But it gets worse. Bill O'Reilly *defended* Tom DeLay. In a clever ploy to soften the criticism against Tom DeLay, O'Reilly brought on Barney Frank, Democratic congressman from Massachusetts, to defend Tom DeLay. Barney Frank, being the fair man he is, had stuck up for Tom DeLay after Howard Dean had said that "Tom DeLay ought to go back to Houston, where he can serve his jail sentence." O'Reilly brought on Barney Frank on his show of May 17, 2005 in a segment entitled "Barney Frank Sticks Up for Tom DeLay" and here is how the conversation went:

> *O'Reilly*: "In the "Personal Story" segment tonight, one of the most outspoken congressmen on the Hill is Barney Frank from Massachusetts, a fiercely dedicated Democrat. Over the weekend, DNC chief Howard Dean said, 'Tom DeLay ought to go back to Houston, where he can serve his jail sentence.' But

Congressman Frank objected to those words. He joins us now from Washington.

Don't you think that Howard Dean is the best friend the Republican Party could ever have, saying all this stuff? I mean, why does he do that?"

Barney Frank: "Well, not all the time. I think we're all told, a lot of us, you've got to energize your base, et cetera, et cetera. And I agree that you really do want to make sure that the people who most strongly support you are enthused.

But I think you have that in a regional way. I guess there are people who think maybe, you know, being tough and being fair are inconsistent.

Governor Dean gets enthusiastic. I don't think he's the Republicans' best friend. I think he's been a very valuable Democrat. But I want to preserve my ability to speak out honestly.

Now, most of the time I'm going to agree with the Democrats and disagree with the Republicans. But on those occasions when I do strongly disagree with the Democrats and I don't say anything, I think I forfeit my right to have people pay attention to me when I say the things that I don't like about what Republicans are saying."

O'Reilly: "Well, did you think it was a cheap shot?"

Barney Frank: "I think it was inappropriate. I'm a great critic of Tom DeLay's. I have nothing personal against him. I think he has run the House in a very bad way. I was very upset with what they did on the Ethics Committee.

But to say that he's a criminal, at this point there's no basis for that. He hasn't been indicted. And yes, I thought it was a very unfair and inappropriate thing to do.

And I also agree, there has been this tendency. People have denounced the criminalization of political debate. It ought to be possible to say that your opponent is a fool and has no idea what he or she is talking about, maybe isn't even well-intentioned in this particular thing, without us trying to throw each other in the slammer."

O'Reilly: "Yes. I mean, I'd like to see the character assassinations stop, as well."

So, Bill O'Reilly wants the character assassinations to stop, do you believe it? Isn't that incredible? Here's a man who has called people the worst names you can think of—pinhead, nut, crazy, radical, loon, and I could go on and on. He allegedly went so far as to say that if Jimmy Carter were still President today we would all be speaking Arabic. And he wants the character assassination to stop? Well, a good place to start is with YOURSELF, Mr. O'Reilly Anyway, getting back to his Tom DeLay coverage, it is just remarkable that a man who parades around as an ethical and moral watchdog against powerful people didn't see a problem with Tom DeLay and didn't call for DeLay to resign. The only reason I can think of why he didn't condemned DeLay was that he didn't want to hurt the Republicans, there is no other reason. I'm convinced that if a Democrat did the same things that DeLay did, O'Reilly would have called for his resignation. He called for Democrat Gary Condit to resign even though Condit wasn't charged with anything. Condit was having an affair with Chandra Levy, a Washington intern who disappeared, but it was never proven that Condit had anything to do with her disappearance. O'Reilly said Condit should resign because he "brought immense pain to the family of Chandra Levy", and went on further to say that "elected officials have a responsibility to set a moral tone."[2] But the problem is that O'Reilly applies this standard only to Democratic politicians. Doesn't Tom DeLay have the responsibility to set a moral tone? With all of the ethical questions swirling around Tom DeLay, why did Bill O'Reilly not call for his resignation?

On the evening of DeLay's indictment, O'Reilly opened his show with analysis of the DeLay situation from *Republican* strategist Kellyanne Conway and pro-Republican Academic Larry Sabato, both of whom went soft on Tom DeLay, and failed to explain the indictment so that people could understand what DeLay was accused of. O'Reilly chose not to put someone on who would have been critical of DeLay or who would have dealt more with the details of the indictment. It was a charade. But worst of all, O'Reilly remarked that on his radio show earlier in the day, only a few people were interested in the story, insinuating that the indictment of DeLay was not a big deal. And O'Reilly himself made no attempt to explain to his viewers what exactly Tom DeLay was accused of, leaving the impression that the charges were murky and questionable, which they were not. O'Reilly also went on to raise questions about the motive of the prosecutor, Ronnie Earle. Clearly, O'Reilly did not want to vilify Tom DeLay, because he knew that it would hurt the Republican Party badly, since Tom DeLay was the Majority Leader at that time and represented the face of the Republican Party. Even more dishonest was O'Reilly's changing standards for judging ethics and morality. He refused to pound Tom DeLay because "he doesn't know how much people are interested in the story".

As I mentioned above, in this same segment with Conway and Sabato, he said that earlier on his radio show only a few people called in to talk about the DeLay indictment, and he expressed doubt that people were outraged by whatever DeLay was accused of. In effect, he was saying that he was going by people's sentiments, which he believed wasn't terribly unfavorable towards Tom DeLay, so he (O'Reilly) will reflect that same sentiment. In this case, O'Reilly's standards of morals and ethics seemed to have been dictated by the polls and public opinion. But that is not usually his standard for pursuing alleged wrong doing by Democrats. With Democrats, he doesn't care whether or not people are interested in the story. He applies black and white ethical and moral standards, and doesn't hesitate to convict. He is usually very specific in pointing out what Democrats are accused of and why he thinks they are dishonest, even before any investigation has begun, and sometimes even after an investigation is complete and finds no wrong doing. The double standard is odious.

George W. Bush versus John Kerry

Bill O'Reilly interviewed George W. Bush just before the 2004 presidential elections, but did not get an interview with John Kerry because Kerry turned down his invitation to appear. The interview with George W. Bush was a "soft ball". O'Reilly looked like a lamb, very untypical of his style, and he bent over backwards so that George W. Bush does not look bad. This is the same man who blasted Jim Lehrer for being soft on Bill Clinton, as I pointed out earlier. It was very obvious that O'Reilly didn't want the interview to hurt Mr. Bush. O'Reilly wasn't confrontational at all, failed to ask tough questions, and didn't insist on straight answers. For example:

1) O'Reilly asked President Bush if he registered for military service when he was in Massachusetts but Bush didn't answer the question, and O'Reilly did not insist on an answer, as he would normally do with Democrats. We still don't know whether Bush registered when he was in Massachusetts, and I'm sure O'Reilly doesn't know either. Here is how the questions and answers went down:

> *O'Reilly*: "They say you didn't register in Massachusetts. Is that bogus?"
> *Bush*: "I fulfilled my duties. I mean, this is—I did exactly what my commanders told me to do."
> *O'Reilly*: "OK. Do you think the swift boat vets' charges against Kerry are unfair?"

So, there you have it, Republican George W. Bush would not give a clear answer to Bill O'Reilly, and O'Reilly does not follow up and insist on getting an answer. Isn't O'Reilly interested in the truth? Doesn't he want to know whether or not Mr. Bush registered in Massachusetts? Well, obviously not, because he doesn't want to embarrass Republican George W. Bush.

On the other hand, since O'Reilly did not get to interview John Kerry, O'Reilly did what he called an "almost" Kerry interview, whereby he invited other people to answer for John Kerry. And you guessed it: the questions were much tougher and much more confrontational. For example, he asked Marianne

Marsh, a Democratic strategist whom he invited on his show to answer for Kerry, the following question:

> "According to the European Journal of International Law 5,000 Kuwaiti women were raped after Saddam Hussein invaded Kuwait in 91. You, Senator Kerry, voted against removing Saddam's forces. Why did you do that? And would you change your vote now that you know 5,000 women were raped? What say you?"
> "To give it more time would have meant more women raped, more Kuwaitis murdered. Estimates up to a thousand murdered. So, while you're waiting for sanctions, people are being raped and murdered, Senator. Would you have done it differently had you known that?"

A very different tone for Democrat John Kerry, isn't it? I guess Senator Kerry was wise not to appear on his show. O'Reilly would have clearly ambushed him and tried to destroy his reputation. And if you see the actual interview with Marianne Marsh on television you'll no doubt see the contrasting style. When he interviewed Mr. Bush he did not ask Mr. Bush about the thousands of Iraqis who were killed and maimed since the 2003 Iraq war started and what Mr. Bush has to say to the families of those people. It sounds fair to me that if you're going to ask one man about how his action led to people suffering you should also ask the other guy too, particularly since more people were killed in the 2003 Iraq war than were killed in the 1991 Gulf War. Isn't that fair? But we all know O'Reilly isn't fair.

2) O'Reilly asked Mr. Bush about illegal immigration and the border situation with Mexico, and Bush's answers were similar to what many Democrats would say, but yet O'Reilly didn't challenge Mr. Bush the way he would normally challenge Democrats on the issue of Immigration:

> *O'Reilly*: "A 'Time' magazine investigation says, 3 million illegal aliens crossed the Mexican border, and we talked about this four and a half years ..."
> *Bush*: "We have. I know it's a issue that you're concerned about."
> *O'Reilly*: "Every year, 3.5 million illegals come over. Why can't the federal government control that?"
> *Bush*: "Well, as you know, as the governor of Texas, I was very aware of this issue. There is a long border that makes it hard to control. We have beefed up places along the border to try to stop the process of ..."
> *O'Reilly*: "With all due respect, though, it's not working, with 3 million ..."
> *Bush*: "It's working a little better. They're doing a pretty good job down in Arizona, which is the main border crossing. But I was trying to get my words

here for a minute. I was trying to give you some facts. I think there's a thousand more border patrol agents along the border, we're modernizing border techniques, we're using better surveillance methods to stop crossing at the border. Now, look, people are coming up because they want to work. You know, family values don't stop at the border."

O'Reilly: "Absolutely".

Bush: "If you can make 50 cents in the interior of Mexico, and five bucks in the interior of the United States, you're coming for the five bucks, and they're poor."

O'Reilly: "Ninety percent of them are, but 10 percent are bad guys."

Bush: "Well, look ..."

O'Reilly: "A lot of bad guys coming here."

Bush: "I don't know how you got the 10 percent number, maybe ..."

O'Reilly: "The border patrol you know, incarceration, violent crime, that ..."

Bush: "No question about it. It is a serious issue. I happen to believe the best way to enhance the border is to have temporary worker cards available for people. And I think it's best for the employers who are employing these people. I think it's best for the employees that are trying to find work. I think the long-term solution for this issue on our border is for Mexico to grow a middle class. That's why I believe in NAFTA ..."

O'Reilly: "We'll be in the grave."

Bush: "I don't think so. It's happening. Look, I wish I could have taken you down there and shown you the northern tier of states in Mexico ten years ago compared to today. I mean, it's happening.

Free trade helps lift lives, free trade develops commerce, free trade gives people a chance to realize their dreams. And so long as the wage differential is as big as it is, and so long as moms and dads feel the necessity to feed their children, they're going to come and try to make a living."

O'Reilly: "So you're not going to militarize the border to stop ..."

Bush: "No, we're going to use the border patrol, beef it up, give it better technologies and better equipment to do its job."

O'Reilly: "OK. You know a lot of people are not going to like that answer, you know that."

Bush: "Well it's a truthful answer."

O'Reilly: "OK."

Bush: "I mean, as opposed as to what, putting a military on the border."

O'Reilly: "Yes, [use the] military to back up the border patrol, to just stop the, rampant ...

Bush: No, I think the best way to do it is to give the border patrol the assets it needs to do its job."

O'Reilly had to have been in vehement disagreement with George W. Bush on Immigration, because in October of 2003 he wrote a piece in the New York

Daily News entitled "Let's Stop Coddling Illegal Aliens", and here is part of what he said:

> "Here's the truth: Presidents Bush, Bill Clinton, George Bush the elder and Ronald Reagan all avoided cracking down on the porous borders for political and economic reasons.
> Businesses like the cheap labor illegals provide, and ethnic pressure groups will brand you as an anti if you scrutinize undocumented aliens.
> As a result, the feds estimate that 8 million people are in this country who shouldn't be.
> …
> One of these days, some terrorist is going to walk across our border and do something dastardly. When the story is exposed, the politicians will raise a hue and cry and promise to fix the problem. Of course, it will be too late for the unlucky Americans who will be dead, but, hey, that's life in the political world.…"[2]

So why didn't O'Reilly challenge Mr. Bush? Answer: he did not want to put Bush on the defensive or make him look bad. O'Reilly challenges everyone else, mostly Democrats, when he disagrees with them, but he chose not to challenge Mr. Bush. And it gets even more disingenuous: In the same article I sighted above, O'Reilly went on to slam Democrat *Howard Dean*, of all people. Now, Howard Dean has never been in the position to change our Immigration policy, but O'Reilly found a way to slap him on the Immigration issue even though George W. Bush is the one who is in charge of immigration policy. Here is what O'Reilly said in the same article:

> "Howard Dean's solution is to give illegals citizenship if they behave and have jobs. But Dean and the other Democratic candidates have no plan to secure the borders. So what we have here is an all-skate. If you can get to America under President Dean, you are an American. And Dean will not stop you from getting here."[3]

There is so much intellectual dishonesty here I don't know where to start. But to sum it up, O'Reilly believes that the US government should put the military on the border. George W. Bush told O'Reilly that he (Bush) would *not* put the military on the border, and O'Reilly doesn't blast him. But O'Reilly blasts Howard Dean for his immigration policy and for being in favor of granting amnesty to illegal aliens, a position not different from that of George W. Bush, by the way. Do you still want more proof that O'Reilly is a Republican partisan?

In the 2004 presidential election season O'Reilly said he was setting up his "Truth Police" to monitor what was being said in the campaign, by both sides, and to point out inaccuracies whenever they occur. He was always quick to critique ads and statements coming out from the Democratic camp directed towards George W. Bush. He constantly lashed out against MoveOn.org, George Soros, and other Democrats who criticized President Bush unfairly in his opinion. Yet, when it came to John Kerry, O'Reilly failed to defend Mr. Kerry on two very important occasions:

i) Republicans misquoted Kerry on terrorism

In a New York Times Magazine article by Matt Bai, Kerry was asked the following:

> "What it would take for Americans to feel safe again?"

And Kerry answered as follows:

> "We have to get back to the place we were, where terrorists are not the focus of our lives, but they're a nuisance. As a former law enforcement person, I know we're never going to end prostitution. We're never going to end illegal gambling. But we're going to reduce it, organized crime, to a level where it isn't on the rise. It isn't threatening people's lives every day, and fundamentally, it's something that you continue to fight, but it's not threatening the fabric of your life."

The Republicans ran wild with Kerry's statement and grossly distorted what he said. They claimed that Senator Kerry equated terrorism with prostitution and gambling, which was an absolute lie. Here are some actual quotes:

1) The then Bush campaign Chairman Marc Raciot, in an appearance on CNN 'Late Edition' told Wolf Blitzer that Kerry said:

> "The war on terrorism is like a nuisance. He equated it to prostitution and gambling, a nuisance activity."

2) The then Republican Party Chairman Ed Gillespie on CBS 'Face the nation' said:

"Terrorism is not a law enforcement matter, as John Kerry repeatedly says. Terrorist activities are not like gambling. Terrorist activities are not like prostitution ..."

3) President Bush himself said that:

"Senator Kerry talked of reducing terrorism to—quote—nuisance—end quote; and compared it to prostitution and illegal gambling."

Now, Kerry *never* compared terrorism to prostitution and illegal gambling, and never said that terrorism is like a nuisance. Read what he said above again. He was asked to describe a scenario where people will feel safe again, and he said that people will feel safe again *when* terrorism is reduced to a nuisance level and doesn't threaten people's every day lives. But where was O'Reilly with his "truth police"? Why did O'Reilly not stick up for John Kerry and condemn the dishonesty of the Republicans? He stuck up for President Bush on many occasions during the campaign when he perceived that Bush was being attacked unfairly. For example, in his October 25, 2004 edition of *The O'Reilly Factor*, O'Reilly sprung to the defense of Mr. Bush when John Kerry sort of attacked Mr. Bush for saying that it was still up in the air whether or not the United States can be fully safe from terrorism:

"Hi, I'm Bill O'Reilly. Thanks for watching us tonight. Bush versus Kerry on terrorism, that is the subject of this evening's 'Talking Points' memo. President Bush talked with Sean Hannity. That interview will be next on 'Hannity & Colmes'. And one of his statements is causing some controversy."

(BEGIN VIDEO CLIP)
George W. Bush: "The 9/11 Commission reports that America is safer under the course of action we've taken but not yet safe. Whether or not we can be ever fully safe is up—you know, is up in the air."
(END VIDEO CLIP)

O'Reilly: "Now you may remember Mr. Bush said almost the same thing on "The Today Show," and it's true. Nobody can predict whether America can fully defeat terrorism. Wait a minute. Nobody except John Kerry."

(BEGIN VIDEO CLIP)
John Kerry: "Now there's a whole new interview. And the president says in this interview 'whether or not we can be fully safe looking out to the future is up in the air.'

Well, let me tell you something, ladies and gentlemen. You make me president of the United States, we're going to win the war on terror. It's not going to be up in the air whether or not we make America safe."
(END VIDEO CLIP)

O'Reilly: "Wow, that's a pretty bold statement, isn't it? But it may be just politics as usual. Let's analyze it.
Terrorists exist all over the world. We all know that, with Islamic fascists being the most treacherous. Since the world will not unite against terrorism, no single country can wipe the menace out. Worldwide cooperation is needed to do that.
Now Senator Kerry believes he can better mobilize foreign nations to engage the war on terror. He really, really believes that. But it's a hope, not a reality. And so is the senator saying that if president, he will defeat the terrorists. It is simply a hope. And that's a memo."

Clearly, O'Reilly was acting as a defender of George W. Bush. But he did not do the same when John Kerry was unfairly attacked as I pointed out above. He went on to even *attack* Kerry for claiming that he (Kerry) can make the United States fully safe. O'Reilly dismissed Kerry's argument as "simply a hope". But wait a minute, on other occasions George W. Bush and his people have claimed that they can wipe out terrorism, but O'Reilly never dismissed their claim as "simply a hope". You see the double standard here? In speeches after speeches George W. Bush, Dick Cheney, and other Republicans have claimed that they can defeat terrorism. In fact, the entire RNC Convention in New York City was about how George W. Bush is the best person to protect the United States against terrorism. But O'Reilly then didn't seem to think that it was "simply a hope". But when John Kerry says he can protect the United States better O'Reilly dismisses it as "simply a hope". It's interesting that in O'Reilly's talking points memo above he says "no single country can wipe the menace out". I happen to think that this is true, so I agree with O'Reilly on this point. But if he really believed what he said, he should really have had more faith in John Kerry defeating terrorism than George W. Bush, since world opinion at that time favored Senator Kerry much more than President Bush, and had Senator Kerry been elected President he (Kerry) would have had much better international cooperation in fighting terrorism than George W. Bush. Polls in England, Germany, France, Canada, Russia, just to name a few, favored John Kerry. So if O'Reilly sincerely believed that "no single country can wipe the menace out" he should have concluded that John Kerry would be able to fight terrorism better than

George W. Bush, instead of dismissing Kerry's statement as "simply a hope". It looks like ideology had the better of O'Reilly, rather than commonsense.

ii) The Swiftboat Veterans For Truth

One of the most scurrilous attacks leveled against John Kerry by the despicable group "Swiftboat Veterans For Truth" was that John Kerry did not deserve his Bronze Star for rescuing Jim Rassmann on March 13, 1969. A member of the group, Larry Thurlow, who didn't serve on the same boat as John Kerry, but was in another boat which was part of the five-boat flotilla that came under attack from the Viet Congs on that day, claimed that John Kerry's boat did not come under enemy fire, suggesting that the story was made up. Incidentally, Larry Thurlow also received a Bronze Star for that same incident on that same day, and Thurlow's citation did state that "all units began receiving enemy small arms and automatic weapons fire from the river banks". Please see Appendix 2A for the full text of the citation. This is the official Navy record. I assume Thurlow must have read his citation at least a few times, because everyone loves to admire their achievements once in a while, don't they? Now, how can he claim that John Kerry's boat did not come under attack, when his own citation said that "all units" came under enemy fire? Either Thurlow is saying:

(1) He never read the citation, so didn't really know what it said, or

(2) He read the citation before and knew that it was wrong, but never made any attempt to correct the record.

Thurlow took the first line. According to a Washington Post article of August 19, 2004, when confronted with the words of his citation Thurlow said:

> "My personal feeling was always that I got the award for coming to the rescue of the boat that was mined. This casts doubt on anybody's awards. It is sickening and disgusting."

So I guess Thurlow was in effect saying that he never really read the citation that was presented to him. But this is hard to believe, and doesn't sound credible to me. It just doesn't sound credible that someone received an award and didn't really know what they were receiving it for. Thurlow looks like a pretty savvy and articulate guy to me, and I don't believe him when he said that he felt that he got the award for something other than what the citation said. Added to that, he is in effect disputing the official Navy account of events. Plus, *all* of the men who served with John Kerry on his boat said that Kerry's boat did come under enemy fire. So where was O'Reilly's "Truth Police" on all this? This was *the* major story during the 2004 presidential campaign. Why didn't O'Reilly investigate this story and drag Thurlow on his show for questioning? On September 7, 2004 O'Reilly did interview John O'Neill, the head of "The Swiftboat Veterans for Truth". You would expect that this issue would have taken front-and-center stage in the interview, but it didn't. O'Reilly should have demanded an explanation from O'Neill as to how Thurlow could now change his story, but O'Reilly did not press the issue. He allowed O'Neill to continue to spin and deceive. In fact, at the end of the interview O'Reilly seemed to agree with O'Neill that it was okay to trash John Kerry and question his medals.

In my opinion the "Swiftboat Veterans For Truth" was one of the most vile and dishonest organization in recent history, and I hope the American public will refuse to tolerate such despicable organizations in the future. These men, such as John O'Neill and Larry Thurlow have no shame, in my view. I believe they are liars, and I base this assessment on the following facts:

—The official U.S. Government record says that there was enemy fire.

—Thurlow's citation, which he held for nearly thirty years, says there was enemy fire.

—Jim Rassman, the man who John Kerry rescued says there was enemy fire.

—Retired Chief Petty Officer Robert E. Lambert, of Eagle Point, Oregon, who got a Bronze Star for pulling Larry Thurlow out of the Bay Hap River that same day says there was enemy fire.

Did O'Reilly confront John O'Neill with these facts? Absolutely not, he was extremely soft on O'Neill and allowed O'Neill to justify everything without proof. O'Neill and "The Swiftboat Veterans For Truth" had, and still have, no evidence to back up their claims, except word of mouth from officers who did NOT serve with John Kerry. And I believe that O'Reilly deliberately did not try to get to the truth, because it would have helped Senator Kerry. So Democrats better be warned—don't depend on O'Reilly to stick up for you, it wouldn't happen.

APPENDIX 2A

Wording of Larry Thurlow's Citation

The President of the United States takes pleasure in presenting the Bronze Star Medal to

LARRY RAYMOND THURLOW
LIEUTENANT (JUNIOR GRADE)
UNITED STATES NAVAL RESERVE

For service as set forth in the following

CITATION

"For heroic achievement while serving with Coastal Division ELEVEN engaged in armed conflict against Viet Cong communists aggressors in An Xuyen Province, Republic of Vietnam on 13 March 1969. Lieutenant (junior grade) THURLOW was serving an Officer in Charge of Inshore Patrol Craft 51, one of five boats conducting a SEA LORDS operation in the Bay Hap river. While exiting the river, a mine detonated under another Inshore Patrol Craft. At the same time, all units began receiving enemy small arms and automatic weapons fire from the river banks. Lieutenant (junior grade) THURLOW immediately directed the coxswain of his boat to assist the damaged Inshore Patrol Craft. Despite enemy bullets flying about him, he leaped aboard the damaged boat and began rendering first aid and assessing damage to the boat. While attending to the forward gunner, he was knocked overboard. He managed to remain afloat until pulled from the water. He quickly radioed for medical evacuation of the wounded and, while still under fire, with complete disregard for his personal safety, returned aboard the damaged Inshore Patrol Craft. Lieutenant (junior grade) THURLOW remained aboard the stricken boat until it had safely cleared the area. His actions and courage in the face of enemy fire were instrumental in the medical evacuation of the wounded and salvaging the damaged Inshore Patrol Craft and were in keeping with the highest traditions of the United States Naval Services."

Lieutenant (junior grade) THURLOW is authorized to wear the Combat "V"

Footnotes to Chapter Two

1) The O'Reilly Factor, Bill O'Reilly, February 18, 2005.

2) The O'Reilly Factor, Bill O'Reilly, July 10, 2001.

3

A Few More Points To Consider

o o o o o o o o o o o o o o o o o o o o o o o o o o o o o o
"You can fool all the people some of the time, and some of the people all the time, but you cannot fool all the people all the time." (Abraham Lincoln)

1) Bill O'Reilly was a Republican, and probably still is

Did you know that Bill O'Reilly was a registered Republican, and he only changed his party affiliation to Independent when he learnt that he was about to be exposed? According to an article in the Washington Post titled "The Life of O'Reilly", dated December 13, 2000, O'Reilly had been a registered Republican since 1994, and only changed his registration to Independent a week before they published the piece on him—December 2000. Seems like O'Reilly learnt that the article was coming out and he scrambled and changed his party affiliation from Republican to Independent in order to avoid embarrassment. Note that this is not just some rumor put out by a "far left smear website" as O'Reilly is fond of saying whenever people expose his deception. This article was researched and published by one of the nation's most reputable newspapers, The Washington Post, and O'Reilly, to my knowledge has not challenged the veracity of the article. So we can assume that the article was accurate in reporting that he was in fact a registered Republican. How on earth then can this man claim to be an Independent, when he changed his political affiliation only because he was about to be exposed, and not because of his convictions? The fact is he was a Republican, and most likely still is a Republican in his heart; it's just that he wouldn't admit to it because he wants people to believe that he is not a political partisan.

O'Reilly claimed that he is really an Independent and always "splits his ticket" and votes for the best person, and the fact that he was a registered Republican was a "clerical" mistake. Well, I have one word for you, O'Reilly: BALONEY.

O'Reilly must really think that the rest of us are stupid. I wonder how many people honestly believe his explanation. Do you? I just don't buy it. It makes perfect sense that O'Reilly was a Republican, doesn't it? His words and his actions correlate to the way a Republican behaves. It explains the underlying right-wing bias that is so prevalent in everything that he says and writes.

His claim to be independent is purely a ploy to try to separate himself from the usual right-wing warriors such as Sean Hannity, Ann Coulter, Rush Limbaugh, and others. He doesn't want to be labeled a right-wing nut, which is really what he is, so he calls himself an Independent and parades around as regular guy who is interested in truth and fairness. I would bet that many of his admirers don't know that he was a registered Republican, because he has been a very good actor and an extremely skillful imposter. In fact, a friend of mine who is a regular viewer of *The O'Reilly Factor* was quite surprised when I broke the news to him that O'Reilly was a registered Republican. I guess it is one of the untold stories in the life of O'Reilly, and it calls into question the Conservative claim of Liberal bias in the media. If there were in fact Liberal bias in the media this story should have been all over the place. It would be interesting to know what percentage of O'Reilly's supporters actually know that he was a registered Republican. But the central point in all of this is the deception on the part of Bill O'Reilly. For a man who crucifies other people for alleged dishonesty and corruption, it is a real travesty that he is allowed to claim the moral high ground when in fact he has been deceiving millions of people about his real political stripes. I actually respect people like Sean Hannity and Ann Coulter much more than Bill O'Reilly, because at least they are honest in admitting that they are Republicans, and you know where they are coming from. But O'Reilly continues to deceive his viewers and listeners by misrepresenting his real ideological allegiance. This is journalistic fraud, and by itself is enough to call into question the credibility and honesty of Bill O'Reilly.

O'Reilly has attacked and smeared almost every major figure in the Democratic Party—Bill Clinton, Hillary Clinton, Al Gore, Tom Daschle, Howard Dean, Terry McCauliff, Ted Kennedy, Jessie Jackson, Nancy Peloci, George Soros, and many more. He has likewise demonized people in Hollywood, but only those that support the Democratic Party. People like Arnold Schwarzenegger & Charleston Heston, for example, get a pass, because they are Republicans. But people like Susan Sarandon, Sean Penn, George Clooney, Barbara Streisand, Michael Moore, and so on, have been demonized on a regular basis. It is interesting that even though Charleston Heston believes in absolutely no form of gun control, O'Reilly does not attack Heston for those views, even though O'Reilly does believe in gun control. Likewise, Arnold Schwarzennegar holds views that are opposed to O'Reilly on some social issues, but O'Reilly does not attack him the same way he attacks Democrats for those same views. Now, none of the Democrats I mentioned above, to my knowledge, has ever been indicted or convicted of a crime in the United States, but yet O'Reilly constantly and repeatedly slimes them as if they were despicable human beings out to make the world an evil place.

On the Republican side, O'Reilly has defended George W. Bush at virtually every juncture. Can you think of an instance when Mr. Bush was under attack and O'Reilly did not jump in to defend him? He has likewise stuck up for other Republicans accused of wrongdoings and made sure that people know that they are "innocent until proven guilty", something he doesn't normally do when Democrats are accused of wrongdoing. Most telling was his refusal to condemn Tom DeLay for his questionable campaign finance activities. O'Reilly was quick to say that Jesse Jackson was using his non-profit organizations to enrich himself, and called on the government to investigate Mr. Jackson's organizations, but he didn't make the same judgment about Tom DeLay, who allegedly funneled over $500,000.00 from his campaign coffers back to his wife and daughter as "fees" for "services". Where is O'Reilly's outrage for what DeLay has done? In addition, as I already pointed out, DeLay was raising funds from energy companies while legislation affecting those companies was being voted on in the Congress, and he was actually reprimanded by his colleagues for other infractions. But O'Reilly didn't seem to care. Why? Well, you know the answer by now.

In nearly every major election, O'Reilly has supported the Republican over the Democrat:
George W. Bush (Republican) over Al Gore (Democrat)
Rick Lazzio (Republican) over Hillary Clinton (Democrat)
Arnold Schwarzenegger (Republican) over Gray Davis (Democratic)
George W. Bush (Republican) over John Kerry (Democrat)
John Thune (Republican) over Tom Daschle (Democrat)

And it's probably safe to say that in future elections we will all be able to easily figure out whom O'Reilly will vote for; wouldn't we? How can someone like this call himself an independent? He will probably say that he supported the above Republican candidates because of policy differences and his belief of what is good for America, i.e. lower taxes, less government spending, etc. But that is precisely

my point. The fact that he favors certain policies (e.g. less spending on social programs, just to name one) and supports political candidates (Republicans) who
believe in such policies, disqualifies him from calling himself an Independent.

His endorsement of John Thune reportedly came on his July 21, 2004 broad-
cast of *The Radio Factor with Bill O'Reilly*. He was running down the list of
speakers at the Democratic National Convention and explaining whether or not
he will cover their speeches. Tom Daschle was scheduled to speak that night, and
when O'Reilly came to saying whether or not he will cover Tom Daschle, he
reportedly said the following:

> "Tom Daschle: Don't care. With all due respect to the senator, we don't have
> any respect for him at all. And we hope he loses in South Dakota. And
> I—really, I stay out of all these races, but you guys listening in South Dakota,
> vote for the other guy. This Daschle's no good."

Wow! But I guess you're not surprised, are you? O'Reilly directly endorsed a
Republican candidate! And O'Reilly says he stay out of races. Really? Well, apart
from the above endorsement of Tom Daschle's opponent, how does he explain
his bashing of Hillary Clinton in the New York 2000 Senate race? In his October
24, 2000 article in World Net Daily, O'Reilly blasted The New York Times for
endorsing Hillary Clinton. He begins:

> "We are living in desperate political times and The New York Times is par-
> tially responsible. On Sunday, Oct. 22, in the year of the Lord 2000, the
> Times editorial page could hold back no longer. Faced with Hillary Clinton's
> falling poll numbers, the dark print screamed out: 'Hillary Clinton for Sen-
> ate'".

He then proceeded to go on a smear campaign against Mrs. Clinton:

> "There is no question that Hillary Clinton is not an entirely honest individual.
> There is no question that she has used her power as first lady to keep the press
> away from her and to campaign with the taxpayers' money; something no
> other candidate can do. According to government investigators, she has con-
> sistently lied under oath and sold access to the White House in return for
> campaign money. These are undeniable facts and they add up to a woman
> who subverted the free-election system. She uses her Secret Service bodyguard
> to prevent media questioning, has flown to campaign events aboard Air Force
> jets, and has raised money by offering accommodations at the White
> House—accommodations that the taxpayers fund and most of us would like

to experience. Yet Howell Raines and millions of other New Yorkers want this woman to be a senator. This sends a chilling message, which is that you can be dishonest and sneaky and vindictive and ruthless—but if you agree with my ideological position, I'll endorse you."

This article contains quite a few of the devices I outlined in Chapter One. There is *Misrepresentation*, *Double Standard*, *Demonization*, and *Fabrication*. For a start, Mrs. Clinton never lied under oath, and was never convicted of anything. She didn't lie or mislead any more than George W. Bush did on Iraq and other issues (as I pointed out in Chapter One). Also, it's interesting how O'Reilly holds Hillary Clinton to a different standard than everyone else in politics. Selling access is done all the time, this is standard American politics, and nearly all politicians do it—grant access in exchange for financial and other support. Why hold Hillary Clinton to different standard? As far as flying in Air Force jets is concerned, she was First Lady at the time and she was entitled to fly on Air Force jets. What was she supposed to do? Take the Amtrack train service? Which political candidate would pass up an opportunity to fly in Air Force jets? I'm sure the campaign finance authorities looked into whether she reimbursed the government appropriately, because she was never charged with any improprieties. You see, these are the types of smear tactics that Bill O'Reilly engages in against Democrats, and he states it like fact. Why should Hillary Clinton not use all the resources available to her to win an election? George W. Bush did. When he was campaigning for re-election is 2004 he flew in Air Force One, didn't he? Nearly everything O'Reilly accused Hillary Clinton of above, George W. Bush is also guilty of—using Air Force jets to campaign, using the secret service to control the media and demonstrators, granting favors for campaign finance, etc., but he never demonized George W. Bush the same way. This is just plain double standard. O'Reilly wants to judge Democrats and people he disagrees with on the strictest standard, but when it comes to Republicans he either ignores their improper tactics or changes the standard.

I need not get into George W. Bush versus Al Gore; we all remember his passionate advocacy for George W. Bush during the Florida recount, so it is pretty obvious who he was rooting for. And I need not get into Arnold Schwarzenegger versus Grey Davis, because I think most of you will remember him branding Grey Davis a liar, unjustifiably in my opinion, and condemning Mr. Davis in the harshest possible terms. I've already documented his bias against John Kerry in Chapter Two.

2) Bill O'Reilly is one of the most vicious smear merchants in America

There is no one in America today, and I mean *no one*, in my opinion, who can smear people as effectively as Bill O'Reilly. He is a real genius at it, and I get a kick out of listening to him when he chastises other people for engaging in smear tactics. It's the classic case of the pot calling the kettle black. It's like listening to Saddam Hussein lashing out at people who torture people. I mean, come on, Bill O'Reilly accusing other people of smear tactics? Here is a man who has built fame and fortune by slinging mud into the faces of people he doesn't like. His television program, his columns, and his books are all littered with smears and innuendo against many good people. O'Reilly is so good that he could take even a sinless man like Pope John Paul II and make him look like the devil. In March 2003 O'Reilly derided and insulted Pope John Paul II for being against the Iraq War. Here is part of an article he wrote that reappears in his book *Who's Looking Out for You*, page 147-49:

"But Pope John Paul is another matter. His opposition to military action is understandable in theory but troubling on practice.

John Paul sent his emissary, Pio Cardinal Laghi, to tell President Bush that attacking Iraq would be unjust and immoral. That's like sending Sister Mary Theresa to tell Eminem to stop cursing. The President is firmly convinced that Saddam is an evil man with murder on his mind. Short of Jesus appearing in the Oval Office with an opposing point of view, Bush is not going to change his opinion.

The Catholic Church embraces the tradition of "just war." That is, any use of force must be accompanied by clear and convincing evidence that only force will solve a situation that is both threatening and immoral. And since there is the possibility that UN weapons inspectors might be able to restrain Saddam, the Pope believes there are still options to war.

The problem with that argument is faith, pardon the pun. The Pope is putting his faith in a system of inspections that very well might fail. If that happens and even a portion of Saddam's unaccounted for 8,500 liters of anthrax is used against people, a worldwide catastrophe would ensue.

The Pope does not answer questions, so it is impossible to know what he thinks about that possibility. We also don't know how John Paul squares keeping Saddam in power, considering his murderous past. It's one thing for the Vatican to condemn Saddam's gassing of the Kurds, mass murder and rape in Kuwait, and funding of suicide bombing expeditions—it is quite another thing to prevent those things.

So what are America's 65 million Catholics supposed to do? Theologically, the Pope is on firm ground. Humanistically, he is one of the many Saddam enablers. If the nations of the world would unite against evil things like Saddam, and the insanity of countries like North Korea, deadly situations would be solved and the world would be a better, safe place.

But the world will not unite against evil, and the Pope does not call for that practical unification. Instead, he calls for peace. Does he really believe Saddam and North Korea's Kim Jong Il are listening?

The Catholic Church teaches *tranquillitas ordinis*, the peace of order, which is supposed to be imposed by legal and political means. But as the world has seen, Osama Bin Laden, Adolf Hitler, and yes, Saddam Hussein have not been bullish on the peace of order. Instead, they have embraced the practice of violent chaos.

As a loyal Catholic, I am glad the Pope is praying for America and for peace. I pray his prayers will work a miracle and Saddam will be removed from power without bloodshed.

But if that miracle is not forthcoming, this Catholic does not have faith that Saddam will not use his outlawed anthrax somewhere down the line.

And so, to prevent the mass death that took place in Europe and Asia while another Pope was praying sixty years ago, I support the moral quest of removing a dangerous killer from power. God forgive me."

Can you believe it? Why does O'Reilly have to mock the Pope and attack the Pope's faith in such a vicious and sarcastic manner simply because the man is against war? It just wasn't necessary. The Pope is not a threat to anyone. O'Reilly claims to be a Christian, so he must know that Jesus preached non-violence. The Pope is a man of God and a man of faith, and he has to follow his beliefs and convictions wherever that takes him, even if it means opposing the United States going to war against Iraq. If O'Reilly disagrees with Jesus he should have the guts to say so. I sometimes feel that if Jesus were alive today, people like O'Reilly and some other Conservatives would be opposed to him. Am I wrong to feel that way? The dictionary defines a Christian as "one who professes belief in the teachings of Jesus Christ". The fact is, like it or not, Jesus opposed the "eye for an eye" philosophy, and instead advocated *offering the other cheek*. Here is what Jesus says in Matthew 5: 38:

> "Ye have heard that it hath been said, an eye for an eye, and a tooth for a tooth: But I say unto you, That ye resist not evil: but whosoever shall smite thee on thy right cheek, turn to him the other also."

So O'Reilly should change his religion and stop calling himself a Christian, because, as I will show later in Chapter Four, people like O'Reilly are against practically everything Jesus stood for. It is beyond me what gives these people the right to call themselves Christians.

Furthermore, the Pope is not being theoretical, as O'Reilly claims. Some of the greatest victories in history have been achieved through non-violence. The Indians, led by Mahatma Gandhi, resisted British colonialism and won independence from the British through non-violence. African Americans, led by Reverend Dr. Martin Luther King, won equal rights in America through non-violence. So non-violence as a means of overcoming conflict is not an impractical concept as O'Reilly argues. Hence, the Pope is on firm ground spiritually and well as practically. O'Reilly is the one who needs to rethink his beliefs. He goes on to mock the Pope for praying and believing in miracles. But aren't praying and believing in miracles basic tenets of being a good Christian? I am surprised that O'Reilly's Christian followers didn't chide him for such mockery of the Christian faith.

So why demonize the Pope for following the teachings of Jesus Christ? Why? The only reason I can think of is ideological: O'Reilly at the time was probably worried about what impact the Pope's opposition to the war will have on public opinion in America. O'Reilly, as I will show throughout this book, looks out primarily for President George W. Bush, and anyone who does anything to adversely affect Mr. Bush will be demonized, the Pope not excluded. My guess is that O'Reilly was fearful that the Pope's anti war stance would resonate with a certain section of the American public, and that would put Mr. Bush in a difficult position. After all, there are over sixty million Catholics in America, and if the vast majority of them sided with the Pope, O'Reilly and Mr. Bush could find themselves in the minority. So demonizing the Pope was *necessary* in order to fight the battle of public opinion. That's my theory. O'Reilly chose to demonize a good man for political reasons. The Pope should never have been dragged into this. What O'Reilly did was vile and reprehensible, and qualifies him as the number one smear merchant in America. If O'Reilly and President Bush had listened to the Pope, we probably wouldn't have been in the mess we're in as far as Iraq is concerned. Don't you think O'Reilly owes the Pope an apology?

3) Bill O'Reilly advocates policies outside of the mainstream, policies that are dangerous, irresponsible, and unworkable.

On September 19, 2001, Bill O'Reilly advocated destroying civilian infrastructure in Afghanistan in an effort to starve the Afghan people and force them to rise up and overthrow the Taliban. Besides the fact that this is grossly inhumane and unfair to millions of innocent people who had nothing to do with Osama Bin Laden, it is a direct contravention of the Geneva Conventions, (Protocol 1, Part IV, Chapter III, Article 54), which says that "starvation of civilians as a method of warfare is prohibited" and "objects indispensable to the survival of the civilian population" are not legal military targets. Hence, had the United States government followed O'Reilly's advise, President George W. Bush could have been accused of crimes against humanity. Thank God no one took his dreadful advice. Here is exactly what O'Reilly said in his September 19, 2001 segment of the *O'Reilly Factor* with his guest Dr. Ken Pollack, deputy director for national-security studies at the Council of Foreign Relations.

> "Now I have said that I—if I were in command of this, I would do pretty much what you said. In fact, I use your column in "The Wall Street Journal" as a reference point because I would—discussed this the day before you wrote. But I would bomb the country, as you said, in strategic ways and hope that the people themselves would rise up and throw the Taliban out because people are starving as it is, and you knock out what little infrastructure they have, they're just not going to have any food because there are only four or five roads in the whole country.
> You can blow—just blow up every truck you see, and then there's not going to be anything to eat. Now is that feasible? Can those people in Afghanistan rise up and throw that government out?"

This wasn't the first time O'Reilly advocated starving civilians. Just two days earlier, in his September 17 program he also said that we should bomb Afghanistan and let the Afghan people starve, and destroy all the airports in Libya and let the Libyans "eat sand". Here is the exact quote:

> "'Talking Points' has studied the Afghan situation. And there should be little wiggle room for the Taliban government. They should be given a short deadline in which to hand over Bin Laden. If they don't, the U.S. should bomb the Afghan infrastructure to rubble—the airport, the power plants, their water facilities, and the roads.
> This is a very primitive country. And taking out their ability to exist day to day will not be hard. Remember, the people of any country are ultimately responsible for the government they have. The Germans were responsible for Hitler. The Afghans are responsible for the Taliban.
> We should not target civilians. But if they don't rise up against this criminal government, they starve, period.
> Next, Iraq must be dealt with. Again, their infrastructure must be destroyed and the population made to endure yet another round of intense pain. I wouldn't invade Iraq. But I would put them out of every possible business. Maybe then the people there will finally overthrow Saddam.

Target three is Libya and Qaddafi. Again, he either quits and goes into exile or we bomb his oil facilities, all of them. And we mind the harbor in Tripoli. Nothing goes in, nothing goes out.
We also destroy all the airports in Libya. Let them eat sand."

"Let them eat sand"—what a maniac. It's hard to believe that someone who graduated from Harvard University thinks and speaks like this; isn't it? He might say that this was just after September 11th and his comments reflected the sentiments at the time given the fact that terrorists had killed 3,000 of our citizens. But should a responsible person like Bill O'Reilly call for the United States to violate the Geneva Convention and put the President of the United States in international legal jeopardy? The statements above are the kind of statements you would expect from uneducated and uninformed people, not from someone who graduated from Harvard. I would hate to think what kind of human being O'Reilly would be if he were uneducated; can you imagine?

The Geneva Conventions is quite clear on the starvation of civilians, either O'Reilly doesn't know what the Geneva Conventions say or he knows and he just doesn't care if the United States violate it or not. We simply cannot listen to someone like this; it will get us into serious trouble. For the record, here is what Protocol 1, Part IV, Chapter III, Article 54 of the Geneva Conventions say:

Art 54. Protection of objects indispensable to the survival of the civilian population
1. Starvation of civilians as a method of warfare is prohibited.
2. It is prohibited to attack, destroy, remove or render useless objects indispensable to the survival of the civilian population, such as food-stuffs, agricultural areas for the production of food-stuffs, crops, livestock, drinking water installations and supplies and irrigation works, for the specific purpose of denying them for their sustenance value to the civilian population or to the adverse Party, whatever the motive, whether in order to starve out civilians, to cause them to move away, or for any other motive.
3. The prohibitions in paragraph 2 shall not apply to such of the objects covered by it as are used by an adverse Party:
(a) as sustenance solely for the members of its armed forces; or
(b) if not as sustenance, then in direct support of military action, provided, however, that in no event shall actions against these objects be taken which may be expected to leave the civilian population with such inadequate food or water as to cause its starvation or force its movement.

As you can see, there is no gray area here; the Geneva Conventions is unequivocal. You can bomb civilian infrastructure only if such structures are being used solely for military purposes. If you knowingly bomb civilian infrastructure knowing that it would hurt civilians, which is what O'Reilly advocated, that is a direct violation of the Geneva Conventions.

Next, we have his campaign against French imports into the United States. As I mentioned previously in Chapter One, he called on his viewers to boycott French product because France did not support the Iraq war. Here is part of his "talking points memo" of March 10, 2003:

> "So 'Talking Points' is about to say good-bye to Roqueford dressing, farewell to Louis Vuitton, au revoir to Yves Saint Laurent. Sorry, guys. We're going to miss you. And say farewell to Pierre Cardin, while you're at it.
> France has now hurt the USA, and for many of us, payback time has arrived."

As I showed previously also, the boycott was a total failure, but the point here again is that O'Reilly seems to have formulated his policy based on knee jerk reaction rather than seriously thinking out the long-term implications of his actions. He just wanted to hurt France, that's it. Like the bully on the block, he is short sighted, just thinking of his immediate urge to inflict pain. It didn't seem to cross his mind that if the French began hurting seriously from a boycott they might in turn start to boycott American products or even impose trade restrictions against American products, and the tit-for-tat could end up hurting America and the world economy. Other countries might join in and start taking sides. The situation could get out of hand and lead to a trade war situation, putting the world economy on a path of recession, all because O'Reilly wanted revenge against the French for not doing what he wants them to do. We simply cannot have people with such mentality formulating public policy in the United States. Trade boycott is one of the most dangerous policies to advocate, because trade works both ways and the world economy depends on trade now more than ever before. In fact, even going back to the 1920's and 1930's, some economists argued that one of the contributing factors to the Great Depression was Protectionism. A trade boycott can have similar effect as Protectionism—one country puts up trade barriers, it affects other countries' exports and unemployment, they in turn react by putting up their own trade barriers in order to control their own imports, and it keeps spreading to other countries. The result is a reduction in world trade, and economies spin into recession. One must think very carefully before advocating a trade boycott, and the reasons for advocating such a measure must be extremely sound and probably be used only as a very last resort. O'Reilly has a far way to go in terms of being knowledgeable enough to formulate public policy. He shouldn't try, because he would only make things worse. It's a good thing that our politicians don't take his advice.

4) Bill O'Reilly lacks the knowledge and expertise required to solve problems

Bill O'Reilly talks, writes and acts with great assurance as if he knows what he's talking about, but most of the time he really doesn't have a clue. He claims to have solutions to all of the problems facing the United States and the world, but it's all just a stunt to convince his viewers and readers that he holds the answers to these complex issues. The fact is that he often lacks fundamental understanding of the problems, and believes that he can solve everything with a right-wing solution. From Economics to Education, to Poverty, to the Drug Problem, Bill O'Reilly has demonstrated his ignorance time and time again by glossing over the issues and pretending that the answers are simple, instead of carefully and methodically working through the issues with knowledgeable people and qualified experts who know what they are talking about.

Let's start with Economics. O'Reilly hammered Alan Greenspan mercilessly in 2000 and 2001 for his handling of the economy. Here is a sampling of his attacks on Mr. Greenspan, taken from *The O'Reilly Factor* edition of July 18, 2001:

> *O'Reilly*: "In the 'Unresolved Problem' segment tonight, if you watch THE FACTOR often, you know that I believe Alan Greenspan contributed mightily to the current economic pullback by keeping interest rates high and money tight last year. Greenspan and the Feds strangled the expansion, and corporate investment dried up, causing commerce to drastically slow down. We're all suffering now because of that, and even though Greenspan and his merry men have cut interest rates six times this year, Wall Street still does not have any confidence in him, and stocks remain under pressure."

As the above statement from O'Reilly demonstrates, he doesn't seem to know anything about Economics and how the economy works. Listening to him is like listening to my five-year old son explaining how the television works. O'Reilly just blames people he doesn't like whenever things don't go well, and his arguments are not based on rational, intellectual reasoning. Above he blames Alan Greenspan. At other times he blamed Bill Clinton. For example, in his May 11, 2001 column in World Net Daily, this is what he said about the economic slowdown:

"The current earnings recession and economic slowdown has its roots in Mr. Clinton's final year in office. During that time, he turned away from managing the economy and devoted a huge amount of time fund-raising for himself (the Clinton Library), his wife's senatorial campaign and the Democratic Party."

So in May of 2001 it was Clinton, then in July 2001 it was Greenspan. I would be interested to hear O'Reilly's opinion as to who was responsible for the slowdown during George H.W. Bush's term in 1989—1992. Bush Sr.?

O'Reilly also seems to have no idea what the function of the Federal Reserve is and how interest rates impact the economy. The Feds raised interest rates incrementally during 2000 because there were fears that the economy was "overheating". Many also felt that stock prices were way overvalued and a gentle slow down was needed. If O'Reilly knows anything about Economics he should know that prosperity comes in cycles, and there is bound to come a time when things slow down a bit; it's not necessarily anyone's fault. This is common to all countries. No one has yet figured out how to keep prosperity going indefinitely at a constant rate. If O'Reilly knows how to do it he should let us know. All he seems to know is how to dramatize things and work people's emotions up against someone. O'Reilly is at his best when he finds a villain. In his ranting above he finds two villains—Clinton and Greenspan—two people he doesn't like anyway, so why not blast them. When you read the above two statements from O'Reilly it gives you the impression that America went through a terrible recession and many people were hurt. But this is all propaganda. Economies go through changes all the time, people are laid off, people are hired and rehired, Companies close, others start up, this is what happens all the time. O'Reilly pretends to be an Economic Expert and tries to take the situation and spin it negatively to cast Mr. Clinton and Mr. Greenspan in a bad light. He clearly is not an Economic Expert and didn't know what he was talking about. The economy came through just fine, and O'Reilly should really apologize to Mr. Greenspan and Mr. Clinton for his unnecessary attacks.

Then we have his solutions to poverty in America, which again demonstrates his fundamental lack of understanding of the problem, and hence his dumb solution. In the aftermath of hurricane Katrina, O'Reilly advocated that it's lessons of the suffering poor be taught in the public schools to every student as a means of instilling in them the importance of getting educated in order to get out of poverty. Here is part of his article of September 9, 2005 published in the New York Post:

"American middle and high school students everywhere should be required to watch videotape of the poor people stranded by Hurricane Katrina. Teachers should point out that many U.S. citizens without the financial means to get out of New Orleans wound up floating face down in the water or, at the very least, were subject to gross indignities and suffering of all kinds.

The teachers should then tell the students that the local, state and federal government bureaucracies failed to protect those poor people even though everybody knew the storm was coming days in advance. The lesson should then segue into how the most powerful nation in the world was powerless to stop 9/11, and scores of other natural and manmade disasters throughout our history. After presenting those undeniable facts, the teachers should then present two questions to the students: Do you want to be poor? And do you believe the U.S. government can protect you if you are poor?"

This sounds good on the face of it, but let's analyze it for a moment. We are talking here about young people around say ages ten to eighteen, who were born in the inner cities, and most of whom likely are already not doing terribly well in school, because they did not get the early learning that is so important to the learning process. Do you think that a lesson in the suffering brought about by hurricane Katrina will suddenly cause them to become more disciplined and responsible? This is fear tactics. Bill O'Reilly's theory is to basically scare kids by showing them horrible things that could happen to them, and that will then cause them to start focusing more on their education. His assumption is that these high school students have the mental pre-requisites and the learning ability in the first place, and all they need is a rude awakening, and that will get them going. But his assumption is not a valid one, and so the entire theory goes down the drain.

If someone doesn't have the mental prerequisites to learn, you can scare them until they wet their pants, and it wouldn't help them to learn anything. Learning is a habit that starts at an early age. It's a skill you develop particularly at the pre-Kindergarten, Kindergarten, and Elementary levels. There are some cases where students have been late learners, but those cases are the exception rather than the rule. Most experts will tell you that early learning is the key. For most of us who have done well academically, our learning ability was cultivated during the early years of our life. In most cases, once a child passes say ten years old, it's hard to change his or her learning habits. I'm not saying it is impossible, but it is very difficult. If you don't help them to develop their learning abilities early, it's extremely difficult for them to be good learners later. So what Bill O'Reilly should be advocating is more Pre-Kindergarten and Kindergarten schools for inner city kids, and maybe mandatory pre-Kindergarten and Kindergarten. But he probably wouldn't do that, because it is not a right-wing solution. It involves spending more money on poor people, an idea that O'Reilly seems to abhor.

Finally, I documented above how O'Reilly scorched the Pope for opposing the Iraq War. This is not the only person, by the way, who O'Reilly has slimed along the way. The list of good and honorable people is a long one. O'Reilly, Mr. Bush, Mr. Cheney, and the other cheerleaders of the war were so certain that invading Iraq was the correct course of action that they were not prepared to listen to anyone else, not even the Pope. O'Reilly himself said that short of Jesus coming down there was nothing else that would have averted the War. Hence, war with Iraq was the undisputable, irrefutable, and unmistakable way forward. And these ideologues were thoroughly convinced beyond a shadow of doubt that everything would work out fine. They know best. They are the ones with the resolve, and people who oppose them are weak and theoretical. Well, time has borne them out to be WRONG. They had no idea what they were getting into. No WMD's were found, and Iraq has become one of the most dangerous places on the face of the planet. The country is tearing apart, and I would argue that in many ways it is worse off now than when Saddam Hussein was in power. So be ware when people like Bill O'Reilly tell you anything with certitude, it is more likely than not that they are wrong. People like him are often inclined to make decisions based on ideology, not on reason and commonsense.

5) Bill O'Reilly tries to win by intimidating his opponents

Let's go back to Canada for a moment. O'Reilly threatened the Canadians with a boycott if they do not do what he wants them to do—send back the two American soldiers who deserted the U.S. army and took refuge in Canada. In the same interview I mentioned previously with the Canadian journalist Heather Mallick, O'Reilly threatened Canada with a U.S. trade boycott that he warned would lead to a recession in Canada:

> *O'Reilly*: "OK. Well, yes. I mean, we've seen, and distressingly so in my opinion, a huge move to the left and for the secular in Canada.
> Now if the government—if your government harbors these two deserter, doesn't send them back ..."
> *Mallick*: "That's right."
> *O'Reilly*: "... there will be a boycott of your country which will hurt your country enormously. France is now feeling that sting. Because Americans believe that freedom of speech is great. Disagreement we respect, but if you start to undermine our war against terrorists, even if you disagree with

it—again, we respect disagreement, if you start to undermine it, then Americans are going to take action. Are you willing to accept that boycott which will hurt your economy drastically?"
Mallick: "I don't think for a moment such a boycott would take place because we are your biggest trading partners."
O'Reilly: "No, it will take place, madam. In France …"
Mallick: "I don' think that your French boycott has done to well …"
O'Reilly: "… they've lost billions of dollars in France according to 'The Paris Business Review.'"
Mallick: "I think that's nonsense."
O'Reilly: "And it will—if you harbor these men, there will be a nationwide boycott. Now not every American will participate, but enough to put your country into a recession."

"Enough to put your country into a recession"—that was O'Reilly's dire warning to the Canadians if they don't do what he wants them to do. Who does this guy think he is? Can you imagine what he would do if he had real power?

On October 25, 2005 O'Reilly urged his viewers to stop patronizing the Progressive Insurance Company because it's owner, Peter Lewis, donates money to the Democratic Party and other Liberal organizations:

"Thanks for staying with us. I'm Bill O'Reilly. In the FACTOR "Investigation" segment tonight, if you can't beat 'em, smear 'em. Far left billionaires George Soros and Peter Lewis who heads the Progressive Insurance Company—remember that, if you have Progressive Insurance, you may want to look elsewhere. Those guys have poured tens of millions of dollars into political organizations designed to harm people with whom the left disagrees."

Clearly, O'Reilly's intention is twofold: one, is to have people cancel their insurance policies with the Progressive Insurance Company so that the company is hurt financially, and two, is to intimidate Peter Lewis to stop donating money to the Liberal groups. This is gangster tactics, isn't it? O'Reilly is acting like a hit man trying to intimidate people into submitting to his will. Why is no one stopping this guy? People should be free to donate money to whomever they want without being threatened by goons such as O'Reilly. And notice how he claims that the organizations that Soros and Lewis support "harm" people. How about right-wing organizations, O'Reilly, do they not similarly "harm" people? And how come you don't threaten people who donate to right-wing smear groups?

During the Christmas season of 2005 O'Reilly whipped up emotions among Christians on the issue of retail stores saying "Happy Holidays" versus "Happy Christmas". O'Reilly doesn't seem to understand that the holiday season actually encompassed four different holidays—Christmas, Hanukah, New Year, and Kwanza. He also doesn't seem to realize that when the clerks in the stores greet customers, the clerks have no way of knowing what religion these people belong to. People don't wear badges saying "Christian" or "Jewish" or "Atheist" or "Muslim", etc. So given the fact that there are four holidays being celebrated around the same time, combined with the fact that store clerks have no way of knowing what holiday(s) each patron celebrates, isn't it a reasonable policy to say "Happy Holidays" rather than "Merry Christmas" in order to be accommodating to everyone? What do you think? Isn't that a reasonable policy? It has nothing to with being anti Christian as O'Reilly wants to have his viewers believe.

A good Christian is not supposed to be offended just because someone says "Happy Holidays" instead of "Merry Christmas". After all, Christianity is not about slogans and banners, is it? In my opinion, O'Reilly and others who made this an issue are phony Christians. These people are not concerned with the substance of Christianity, which is, according to Jesus, mainly about caring for the less fortunate, and treating others as you would want them to treat you. They don't want to deal with issues such as helping the poor and needy, so they latch on to these superficial issues and use them to fire up misguided Christians in order to strengthen their base. This is what this controversy was all about. People like Bill O'Reilly, John Gibson, and others, wanted to set themselves up as heroes for Christians under siege. But the reality is that no one is persecuting Christians, it's a phony issue.

O'Reilly used the issue to threaten stores owners who had a policy of saying "Happy Holidays" into changing their policy to say "Merry Christmas". On almost a nightly basis he publicly named the stores that did and the stores that did not comply with his demands, with the intention of persuading people not to patronizing these stores, and also to intimidate the management of these stores to change their policy. Can you imagine the chaos that would ensue if other people with power and influence act like O'Reilly and call for boycotts and other actions whenever they disagree with other people? It will be total anarchy.

6) Bill O'Reilly demonizes people instead of debating the substance of the issues

There is a difference between debating the ideas, views, and actions of a person, versus demonizing that person in an attempt to cause people to question his or her character. Bill O'Reilly is a genius at the latter, and what this does is it distorts people's perceptions of the facts and causes people to focus on the individual instead of on the issue. When O'Reilly knows he cannot win on the ideas, he resorts to labeling people and bringing in extraneous information to try to damage people's reputation and make them less favorable. Protestors against the Iraq war, for example, are labeled "Far Left", "Left wing loons", "Radicals", "Bomb Throwers", etc. Politicians who believe in helping the poor are called "Socialists", "Left Wing Nuts", "Charlatans", etc. People who oppose the government imposing religion on their children are branded "Secular Left", "Secular Progressives", "Secularist", etc., when in fact these are not secular people but people who are religious but just don't want the *government* getting involved in religion. People who donate large amounts of money to the Democratic Party are "pushing the left wing agenda". And I could go on and on. O'Reilly's objective here is clear and simple: Attach a left wing label to the person in question and in the process make his or her ideas and views sound Communistic. He plays upon people's fear and dislike of Communism from back in the days of the Cold War.

Take the case of Cindy Sheehan, for example, a Mom who lost her son fighting in Iraq, and subsequently became involved with anti-war protests. Instead of debating the merits and demerits of the Iraq war and the case for "staying the course" versus some form of withdrawal, O'Reilly demonizes her and marginalizes her. He puts her in a camp with the "far left" and seeks to establish her left wing "credentials" in order to prove that she has left wing beliefs. So what if she is from the far left? Does that make her less of a human being? Does that diminish her credibility? Does she have to be a Conservative protesting the war in order to be credible? Clearly, there is no intellectual value to bringing in her political beliefs into the issue of whether or not the Iraq war was right or not, or whether the U.S. should pull out at some point. The fact is that she had a son who was in the U.S. military and was killed in Iraq. The woman didn't make this up, and she shouldn't be demonized for legitimately protesting the war. Whether or not she is associating with some left wing individuals makes no difference. What Bill O'Reilly does is he seeks to de-legitimize her activities simply because she is in the company some left wing people. Here is a sampling of Bill O'Reilly's commentary on Cindy Sheehan. Notice how many times he uses words such as "far left", and how he tries to connect Sheehan to left wing people, as if left wing people are the scum of the earth. He also invokes Michael Moore repeatedly as if Michael Moore is a Hitler or a Stalin. O'Reilly seems to believe that by using these words often enough he can damage someone's reputation:

The O'Reilly Factor, Aug 10, 2005:
"There's no question that **far left** ideologues are controlling access to Cindy Sheehan, who you may remember is camped outside of the president's house in Crawford, Texas, wanting to meet with him.
Sheehan is also using **Michael Moore's** Web site to get her **anti-Bush** message out. Well, now we continue to support her right to say whatever she wants to say. After all, she did lose a son in Iraq. But certainly it is our responsibility to tell you exactly who Cindy Sheehan's associating with.
But other media don't see it that way. In her column today, New York Times pundit Maureen Dowd glorified Mrs. Sheehan, but made no mention of **Mr. Moore or other radicals** involved with her."

"And Cindy Sheehan is now an **anti-Bush** woman. So why would he meet with her again? If you were Mr. Bush, would you sit down with someone blogging on the **Michael Moore** Web site? Come on."

"I think she's being used by **very far left elements** in this country, elements that not only object to the Iraq War, but object to basically our way of life here, America as we know it."

"But if you don't believe me, all you have to do is go to the **Michael Moore** Web site. And all you have to do is call the **Fenton Group, which is a left-wing group in Washington**, which puts out press releases.
And here I have an Internet thing where she told us—I mean, these people are **off the chart left**. Cindy Sheehan says Bill O'Reilly is an obscenity to humanity. OK?
But we have **Michael Moore** involved. You know **Michael Moore**."

"We have **the most far left elements** in the country involved with telling the woman what to say, how to say it, and monitoring what she goes on and what she doesn't go on. You know, there's nothing else I can tell you."

On the same program O'Reilly interviewed Delores Kesterson who also lost a son in Iraq and who supports Cindy Sheehan. O'Reilly tried desperately to get her to denounce Sheehan by demonize Sheehan and connecting her to Michael Moore and other left wing individuals and groups, but Delores Kesterson would have none of it. Here is part of the conversation:

O'Reilly: "Would you go on the **Michael Moore** Web site, madam?"
Kesterson: "Probably. I mean, I will now. I mean, I don't go do that, you know, voluntarily, but you know …"

> *O'Reilly*: "But I mean, do you respect **Michael Moore**? Do you believe in the things that **Michael Moore** believes in, that we're a bad country, that we're an evil country …"
> *Kesterson*: "Now see, you're putting words in …"
> *O'Reilly*: "… that we brought this war upon ourselves?"
> *Kesterson*: "You're putting words in his mouth the way I look at it."
> *O'Reilly*: "OK, so you don't—you believe—well, wait …"
> *Kesterson*: "I believe he has made a documentary."
> *O'Reilly*: "Hold it."
> *Kesterson*: "Mm-hmm. Go ahead."
> *O'Reilly*: "Do you respect **Michael Moore's** view of the United States?"
> *Kesterson*: "I don't know his entire views of the United States.
> But you know, there are a lot of things that Michael Moore has brought up that I think needed to be brought up. And I do believe them. But I can't say because I don't know what he has, you know, said across the board. I don't follow him."
> *O'Reilly*: "If you had to throw in with one person, President Bush or **Michael Moore**, if you had to make a decision on who I'm going to back here, who would it be?"
> *Kesterson*: "Michael Moore, if he has lied or not, has not killed thousands of people, possibly hundreds of thousands of people."

Notice how O'Reilly presented the choice to Ms. Kesterson—if you had to choose President Bush or Michael Moore who would you choose. This is surely a tactic of desperation. I guess he was bitterly disappointed that Ms. Kesterson chose Michael Moore. I give her a lot of credit for standing up to Bill O'Reilly and his bullying tactics.

Bill O'Reilly continued his onslaught against Cindy Sheehan a few days later. On his August 15 show he interviewed Joe Trippi, former campaign manager for the Howard Dean presidential campaign, and here is some of what he said. Again, he tried his best to damage Sheehan's reputation using the same types of words and phrases:

> "I don't have any problem with that. But I have a problem with her disguising a protest because **she is a rank political activist**. She has joined the **far left**. You wouldn't deny that, would you?"

> "And then you just said you don't think she's joined the **far left**. Let me quote to you a couple of things from her blog on **Michael Moore**."

"You, Mr. Trippi, are going to sit there and you are smart, sophisticated guy, and tell me you don't believe this is **far left stuff**?"

"And I said to you she partnered up with the **far left**. And you said."

"OK. And that's fine. But you don't believe she's a member of the **far left** right now? You don't believe that?"

"Absolutely. And I can rightly describe her as a **far-left radical**."

And O'Reilly went on to call Sheehan a liar, which he later retracted:

"She has mischaracterized the meeting. She either **lied** then or she's **lying** now."

The meeting in question was a meeting Sheehan and some other military families who lost children in the Iraq war had with President Bush in the summer of 2004, and Sheehan was quoted after the meeting as saying the following about Bush: "I now know he's sincere about wanting freedom for the Iraqis. I know he's sorry and feels some pain for our loss. And I know he's a man of faith." O'Reilly's argument is that if that was how Cindy Sheehan felt back then, and a year later she feels differently, then she must be lying either then or now. But as Cindy Sheehan explained later, "We had decided not to criticize the president then because during that meeting he assured us 'this is not political'. And I believed him. Then during the Republican National Convention, he exploited those meetings to justify what he was doing".

It sounds to me like Sheehan was the one who was misled.

4

Who Is A Christian?

The dictionary defines a *Christian* as "one who professes belief in the teachings of Jesus Christ". Conservatives like Bill O'Reilly and others call themselves Christians, so they should believe in and follow the teachings of Jesus, right? Well, you would think so. But the fact is that Conservatives reject some of the most basic and important teachings of Jesus Christ, teachings which Liberals actually embrace, by the way. It thus makes one wonders what gives Conservatives the right to call themselves Christians, and why do they feel embolden to raise questions about the faith of Liberals, who in my opinion are good Christians based on the true definition of the word. There are five critically important areas in which the teachings of Jesus Christ are diametrically opposed to the beliefs and actions of Conservatives, and this in my opinion raises the question of whether or not Conservatives should be calling themselves Christians in the first place. Because, if being a Christian is about following the teachings of Jesus Christ, but you don't believe or follow his teachings, why would you want to call yourself a Christian? If Bill O'Reilly and his Conservative friends believe that the teaching of Jesus is too theoretical and wouldn't work in the real world, then they should have the guts to say so, find something else to follow, and stop calling themselves Christians, don't you think? Here are the five important areas in which Conservatives, in my analysis, have practically rejected the teachings of Jesus:

1) Helping The Poor And Needy

A constantly recurring theme in the teachings of Jesus Christ is compassion towards the poor and needy. Jesus often criticized the rich for their selfishness and their ambivalence towards the poor and needy, and he himself always showed great compassion towards those who are poor and needy. In Luke Chapter 18, a Ruler asked Jesus what he (the Ruler) needed to do in order to inherit eternal life. He told Jesus that he kept all the commandments and lived a good life, and wondered what else he must do in order to go to heaven. And Jesus answered him that if he wanted to be perfect, he should sell all of his possessions and distribute it to the poor. Of course, the ruler, just like the rest of us, couldn't bring himself to doing that and went away disappointed and sorrowful, because he was a wealthy man and couldn't stand the thought of giving up his comfortable life-style, *even though that would have earned him a place in heaven.* Jesus then went on to tell his disciples that it is difficult for a rich man to go to heaven:

> "And when Jesus saw that he was very sorrowful, he said, How hardly shall they that have riches enter into the kingdom of God!
> It is easier for a camel to through a needle's eye, than for a rich man to enter into the kingdom of God."[1]

Then we have the story about Lazarus and the rich man. Jesus liked to explain concepts and ideas by telling parables in order to get people to better understand his teachings. In Luke 16 he told the parable about a man named Lazarus who went to beg at the door of a rich man. The rich man couldn't be bothered to give Lazarus anything and Lazarus had to gather up the crumbs that fell from the rich man's table. Lazarus died and went to heaven, the rich man died but he went to hell. It's a simple but powerful story:

> "There was a certain rich man, which was clothed in purple and fine linen, and fared sumptuously every day:
> And there was a certain beggar named Lazarus, which was laid at his gate, full of sores.
> And desiring to be fed with the crumbs which fell from the rich man's table: moreover the dogs came and licked his sores.
> And it came to pass, that the beggar died, and was carried by the angels into Abraham's bosom: the rich man also died and was buried;
> And in hell he lift up his eyes, being in torments, and seeth Abraham afar off, and Lazarus in his bosom.
> And he cried and said, Father Abraham, have mercy on me, and send Lazarus, that he may dip the tip of his finger in water, and cool my tongue; for I am tormented in this flame.
> But Abraham said, Son, remember that thou in thy lifetime receivedst good things, and likewise Lazarus evil things; but now he is comforted, and thou art tormented."[2]

The central point in the above passages from the Bible is Jesus **linking eternal life with caring for the poor and needy**. Jesus was very blunt about it. In both cases he was very harsh on the rich for not wanting to help poor and suffering people, and in both cases he explicitly states that rich and selfish people who do not help the poor have no place in heaven. In Matthew 25 Jesus went on to describe the judgment process which, again, he said was mainly about whether or not we feed the hungry, clothe the naked and give shelter to the homeless:

> "When the Son of Man comes in his glory, and all the angels with him, then he will sit on his glorious throne. Before him will be gathered all nations, and he will separate them one from another as a shepherd separates the sheep from the goats, and he will place the sheep at his right hand, but the goats at the left. Then the King will say to those at his right hand, 'Come, O blessed of my Father, inherit the kingdom prepared for you from the foundation of the world; for I was hungry and you gave me food, I was thirsty and you gave me drink, I was a stranger and you welcomed me, I was naked and you clothed me, I was sick and you visited me, I was in prison and you came to me.' Then the righteous will answer him, 'Lord, when did we see thee hungry and feed thee, or thirsty and give thee drink? And when did we see thee a stranger and welcome thee, or naked and clothe thee? And when did we see thee sick or in prison and visit thee?' And the King will answer them, 'Truly, I say to you, as you did it to one of the least of these my brethren, you did it onto me.' Then he will say to those at his left hand, 'Depart from me, you cursed, into the eternal fire prepared for the devil and his angels; for I was hungry and you gave me no food, I was thirsty and you gave me no drink, I was a stranger and you did not welcome me, naked and you did not clothe me, sick and in prison and you did not visit me.' Then they also will answer, 'Lord, when did we see thee hungry or thirsty or a stranger or naked or sick or in prison, and did not minister to thee?' Then he will answer them, 'Truly, I say to you, as you did it not to one of the least of these, you did it not to me.' And they will go away into eternal punishment, but the righteous into eternal life."[3]

Here in Matthew 25, Jesus essentially explains the judgment process in a nutshell. This is undoubtedly one of the most important passages in the Bible, because in addition to instructing us on how we should treat the least fortunate in our society, it also speaks to the very heart of what one has to do in order to inherit eternal life. It overtly connects caring for the least fortunate with Judgment. If someone calls himself or herself a Christian, he or she probably should know this passage by heart, since the message here from Jesus is so blunt and to the point. Jesus basically says that those who take care of the poor and needy will inherit the kingdom of God, but those who don't will be put away into eternal punishment. It's that plain and simple. You can't spin it any other way. Conservatives will probably accuse me of selectively quoting the Bible, but I'm not. As I established in the opening sentences of this Chapter, a Christian is one who believes in the teachings of JESUS. So let's not confuse the issue by bringing in arcane Old Testament stuff. Either you believe what Jesus says, or you don't. If Conservatives cannot find somewhere in the Gospel where Jesus says something different from what I quoted above, then they have to accept it if they truly believe in Jesus. One cannot say that one believes in Jesus and then ignores his teachings and follows something else.

Conservatives don't seem to believe that people who have are under any obligation to help those who do not have. Bill O'Reilly calls helping the poor "Socialism". So I guess if Jesus were alive today O'Reilly would call him a "Socialist", right? He and many conservatives certainly don't seem to believe that Christianity compels them to help the poor. If it were up to Conservatives, America would have been a more sharply polarized society today, where you have extremely wealthy individuals on one side, and a high proportion of very poor people on the other side. Conservatives believe in the concentration of wealth and power, instead of opening up the system and making it a more level playing field for the people at the bottom and the middle. For them, it is more important to protect their interests and their wealthy buddies than helping millions of people get out of poverty. For example, one of the things that I never understood is Republicans' resistance to raising the minimum wage. Here is something that would help lift millions of poor Americans out of poverty, but Republicans don't want to hear about it. And these poor people deserve a raise more than anyone else. They work extremely hard and have very little control over their jobs. Their last raise was since 1996 when Bill Clinton—God bless his soul—pushed through a raise from $4.25 per hour to $5.15 per hour. Only a few Republicans voted for the legislation. Republican politicians and right-wing Economists, along with greedy businesspeople, cried out that the rise in the minimum wage would lead to higher unemployment among the poor. These people claimed at the time that they have the interest of the poor at heart, and used that argument to justify not giving an increase to the poorest and most hard working people in the country. This kind of reminds me of the time when Ronald Reagan and Margaret Thatcher defended their position of not wanting to impose sanctions on the racist South African regime, because they claimed the sanctions would hurt the black people, when in fact what Reagan and Thatcher were doing was protecting white business interests in South Africa.

In the United States, unemployment actually decreased after the minimum wage went up in 1996. The critics were dumbfounded. The theory that increasing the minimum wage leads to higher unemployment among poor people was turned upside down. But this doesn't seem to stop the right-wingers from bringing it up every time the issue of raising the minimum wage resurfaces. They haven't yet woken up and realized that it is really just a textbook theory, nothing else. The reason for the failure of the theory is pretty simple: if you increase the minimum wage it gives people more incentive to work. Those who previously felt that the pay wasn't good now have an incentive to go to work. More people will turn out to work and they will work harder and longer hours, leading to more growth and higher employment. Conservative somehow believe that when you give the rich tax cuts they work harder and produce more, but they don't seem to believe that the same logic applies to poor people—pay them more and they will turn out to work and work harder.

Conservatives may say to me that they support private charity, and that demonstrates their commitment to helping the poor. But that is a red herring argument. The fact is that private charities alone cannot deal with the poverty situation in the United States. If you go back to the era prior to President Lyndon Johnson's so-called Great Society Programs, you will see that there was poverty on a much larger scale that what we have now. Had it not been for these government programs, things would have gotten much worse. Private charities are good, but unfortunately they don't have the resources necessary to fight poverty on a massive scale. If you take the government of the picture, there will be chaos on a grand scale. So the Conservative argument that if the government stays out, private charities will take care of the situation, is simply not supported by history.

Conservative politicians have practically fought against every government measure to improve the livelihood of poor people; you name it—minimum wage increase, spending for education, spending for health care, etc. Their standard defense is that they support private charity helping the needy, and it is not the government's job to "redistribute income" or "redistribute wealth". But the distinction they make between private charity and the government in the context of helping the poor and needy is a false distinction. As a public official, you cannot dump your convictions and call yourself "The Government" when you're making decisions. The government is not an abstract body; it is made up of human beings, elected or nominated to make decisions and laws that govern our lives. Are Republicans saying that when it comes to helping the poor, as a public official, you are supposed to be ambivalent towards helping them, and not let your conviction shape your public policy or your judicial decision? This is strange, because Republicans are always the first to inject "values" into political campaigns and debates, and often use it to project moral superiority over Democrats. They are not afraid to let their personal convictions on certain issues spill over into their politics, and they have no qualms about injecting those personal convictions into their legislative agenda. Their personal convictions on abortion, capital punishment, gay rights, gun control, etc. always influence their legislative agenda, or executive actions, or judicial decisions, but somehow their personal conviction on helping the poor (if they have one) doesn't seem to shape their thinking at all. I don't understand how you can be a public official with executive, legislative, or judicial power, have a conviction for helping the poor, but don't let that conviction influence you in your actions, but yet your convictions on abortion, capital punishment, gay right, etc. shape nearly every other decision you make. So I have to ask Conservatives the following questions:

1) Do you really care for the poor and less fortunate in our society?

2) If you do, how come your caring doesn't manifest itself in your public policy? Abortion spills over from your private belief into your policy making, gay rights issues spills over from your private belief into your policy making, same thing with gun control and taxes, but when it comes to your commitment to helping the poor it is not reflected in your public policy at all.

So one has to conclude that Conservatives' commitment to helping the poor is not genuine, because we don't see any passion for helping the poor in their public policy making the same way we see their passion against abortion, gay rights, gun control and taxes. Tell me where I am wrong.

My personal belief is that Conservative Republicans simply don't care about poor and needy people, because these people are not part of their constituency. Republicans by and large don't depend on poor people for votes or political campaign contributions, so why should they bother to help poor people? I have no problem with Republicans if they believe that poor people should be left to fend for themselves. It's a free country, and people are free to believe whatever they wish. But what I do have a problem with is people with these beliefs, like Bill O'Reilly, claiming to be Christians, and questioning the faith of others who actually believe in Jesus' call to help the poor and needy.

O'Reilly often refers to people on the left as "secular progressives"; so I guess he is implying that his standard of Godliness is in some way higher than these "secular progressives". But he never explains to his viewers what is the meaning of being a Christian and what makes him a better Christian than these "secular progressives". He doesn't tell his audience that these "secular progressives" actually believe strongly in helping the poor and needy, which is the core of Christianity. And he also doesn't tell them that Conservatives, in the main, do not believe in large-scale efforts to help the poor and needy, which is actually an anti-Christian position based on the definition of who a Christian is. So you can decide for yourself who are the real Christians here: O'Reilly and his Conservative crowd, or the "secular progressives" as O'Reilly likes to call them.

I also often wonder what Conservatives think about someone like Mother Theresa, and how they square her passion for helping the poor and needy with their own meanness and their individualistic approach towards their fellow human beings. Here is a woman who gave up everything to be with and help the poor and suffering in one of the poorest areas of the world. It is clear that the moral position of Mother Theresa is vastly superior to that of Conservative Christians, both in terms of her Christian philosophy and her deeds. There is a real clash of Christian beliefs here that ought not to be ignored. Mother Theresa's approach to the concept of Christianity is actually diametrically opposed to that of Conservatives in many areas, particularly in the area of helping the poor and needy. Why then do we allow Conservatives to claim moral superiority over the rest of us, when clearly they are morally deficient in key areas of Christianity?

Finally, one of the things that really bother me is when Conservatives mock people who show compassion for the poor. Such people are sarcastically called "do-gooders" or "liberal do-gooders". They are talked about as if they are doing something evil, and are sometimes branded "Socialists", or even "Communists". I find it hard to understand how Conservatives, who call themselves "Christians", can engage in such attacks on people who are only doing what Jesus preached—caring for the poor and needy. It is a really sickening situation that I find very hard to understand, particularly when Conservatives claim that America is a "Christian" country. What exactly is their concept of "Christianity"? I ask.

2) Peace and non-violence

Just in case some Conservatives are not familiar with Jesus' teachings about "offering the other cheek" in the context of violence directed towards us, here is the full text of what Jesus had to say regarding the subject:

> "But I say unto you, that ye resist not evil: but whosoever shall smite thee on thy right cheek, turn to him the other also. And if any man will sue thee at the law, and take away thy coat, let him have thy cloak also. And whosoever shall compel thee to go a mile, go with him twain. Give to him that asketh thee, and from him that would borrow of thee turn not thou away. Ye have heard that it hath been said, Thou shalt love thy neighbor, and hate thy enemy. But I say unto you, love your enemies, bless them that curse you, and do good to them that hate you, and pray for them which despitefully use you and perse-cute you."[4]

At this point, Conservatives like Bill O'Reilly will probably say that the above is not practical, and we cannot possibly expect anyone to follow it exactly. They will argue that no one can possibly follow this teaching because they will be taken advantage of and will never get ahead in life. If that is their argument, then here are my questions: What is the point of having a Bible and talking about Jesus and Christianity if you cannot follow what Jesus taught? Why did Jesus put forth these teachings? Was he just being stylish? Furthermore, if you cannot or would not follow the teachings of Jesus because you think it is impractical, why are you even calling yourself a Christian to begin with? Again, as I noted in the beginning, a Christian is one who *professes belief in the teachings of Jesus Christ*. What gives Conservatives the right to call themselves Christians if they are ignoring the teachings of Jesus?

Conservatives, in this instance also, actually believe in the opposite of what Jesus taught. They believe in lots of guns, big armies and abundant armaments. They have no patience for negotiations and don't like to talk to their "enemies". They believe in power through strength rather than power through consensus and compromise. Again, they have the right to hold those positions and act accordingly, and I don't want to take that right away from them or have them change their beliefs. But what I have a big problem with is their denigration and demonization of people who believe in peace and non-violence. I already documented O'Reilly's contempt for Pope John Paul II in the context of the Pope's opposition to the Iraq War. This is a classic case of the perversion of Christianity: people who follow the teachings of Jesus are mocked and ridiculed by those who oppose good Christian values but call themselves Christians anyway.

I also documented how non-violence can overcome serious conflicts, as in the case of Reverend Martin Luther King Jr. and Mahatma Gandhi leading their people to victory without violence. So offering the other cheek is not an impractical idea. It has worked in the past and it could work in some case in the future if there is good leadership. Clearly, the concept should not be denigrated and the people who believe in the concept should not be marginalized. It is time for Conservatives to admit that *they* are on the wrong side of these issues rather than attack those who are the true believers. They often attack real Christians such as Quaker Groups and Peace Activists, and try to portray these people as unpatriotic and un-American. This is unchristian, and Conservatives need to examine their own consciences and reassess their beliefs.

3) Capital Punishment

One of the basic tenets of Conservatism is the death penalty. I don't know of a prominent Conservative who opposes the death penalty on moral or religious grounds; it is just not part of their Christian ethics. President George W. Bush, a

Conservative, and former Governor of Texas, has been one of most prolific exe-
cutioners in recent American history. During his tenure as Governor of Texas, a
record 152 persons were executed. Many people might be upset that I use the
word "executioner", but I believe that its use is valid in this particular case, and
here is why: As a Governor, you have the power to stop any execution. You can
even impose a moratorium on executions, as Governor George Ryan did in Illi-
nois, and stop all executions. So if a Governor *chooses* NOT to exercise that
power, then he or she is the one who bears ultimate responsibility for the execution in question. Now, I'm not going to be a partisan on this issue. **I believe that
Democrats and others who support the death penalty are also wrong and
should rethink their position**.

The Sixth Commandment (Thou shall not kill) is emphatic and unambigu-
ous; there are no caveats or footnotes, and Jesus reaffirms that whoever kills shall
be liable to judgment.

> "You have heard that it was said to the men of old, 'You shall not kill; and
> whoever kills shall be liable to judgment.'"[5]

Now we all agree that in some cases, like self-defense and wars, we simply have
no choice, because either we die or we kill the enemy. So I don't want to dema-
gogue the issue. But capital punishment is particularly egregious because it is
cold-blooded murder, plain and simple. The government and it's people, in a
misguided quest for "justice", systematically and deliberately decides, in a rational
and methodical manner, that someone who is already in custody in chains and
behind bars, and could be kept there for the remainder of his or her physical life,
should be murdered on a certain date, at a certain time, by a certain person, in a
certain place. It is awful, it is sinful, and it is un-Christian, in my view. It's the
ultimate punishment that was meted out to Jesus Christ by people who possessed
a misguided sense of justice. It's the same thing the terrorists do when they
behead their hostages. They plan the execution, set a date, a time, and a manner
in which the captive should die, and even video tapes the event. What is the difference in principle and methodology between the United States Government (or
any other government for that matter) executing its citizens, and Al Qaeda executing its hostages? Or to make it easier to understand, what are the similarities?
1) Both agree that someone deserves to die.
2) Both agree that killing someone is okay in the eyes of God.
3) Both plan their execution with meticulous detail—date and time, place, manner, etc. In the USA even the last meal of the prisoner is planned.

Now, the *reason* for the execution is different in the case of say the United States versus that of an execution carried out by a terrorist organization. In the United States we have a trial by jury and there is an appeal process that must be exhausted before someone is executed. We can also argue whether or not the trial is fair, but that is beside the point. We will assume for argument sake that the trial is fair and the person in question is guilty without a doubt. On the other hand, in the case of terrorists carrying out an execution, there is obviously no trial and no fairness whatsoever. So the difference between the two is that in the United States we have a fair trial whereas in the case of the terrorists we don't. But as Christians, are we supposed to execute people even if we are one hundred percent certain that they are guilty? I challenge any Conservative, or anyone else for that matter, to show me something that indicates that Jesus would have supported the death penalty. Based on everything that is written in the Gospel, it is crystal clear that Jesus would have emphatically opposed the death penalty. Therefore, if someone calls himself or herself a "Christian", he or she must follow Jesus and oppose the death penalty.

Bill O'Reilly, by the way, says he oppose the death penalty. However, he opposes it not because he thinks it is too barbaric, but because he thinks it is *not barbaric enough*. He believes that the convicted person gets off too lightly by being put to death, and should instead be sentenced to life imprisonment and be required to suffer harshly for the rest of his or her life. In a June 14, 2001 article entitled "Work or Die", O'Reilly argued that the death penalty was too lenient a punishment for killers like Timothy McVeigh. Here is part of what O'Reilly says in that article:

> "… So here's a better way. Killers, rapists, drug kingpins and terrorists should all be subjected to life in prison without parole in a federal work camp. This special prison system would be run military style and be located on federal land in Alaska. It would be in effect a gulag.
> Here the worst criminals in the country would be banished and forced to labor eight hours a day, six days a week in the harsh climate. They would be denied television, computers, exercise equipment (as if they'd need it) and most other "comfort" items. Their mail would be screened, and they would only be allowed a few visitors per year. If the criminal would not cooperate with the work detail, his food rations would be cut, and he would be placed in solitary confinement.
> Now let me ask you, is that not a worse punishment than Timothy McVeigh received? His lawyer actually told the press that McVeigh preferred the lethal injection to spending his life in prison.…

Timothy McVeigh killed 168 people but did not suffer a painful death. His lethal drip contained a sedative along with poison. McVeigh would have suffered far more in a work camp ..."[6]

I don't know about you, but when I read stuff like this coming from someone who calls himself a Christian, I know right away that this person has a very long way to go in terms of being an actual Christian. Calling yourself a Christian doesn't necessarily mean that you are a Christian. Anyone can call them self anything. I can call myself a pacifist, but if I don't follow the principles of Mahatma Gandhi and Dr. Martin Luther King Jr., I'm not really a pacifist. So Bill O'Reilly and other Conservatives are free to call themselves Christians, but it doesn't mean that they are actually Christians. A Christian certainly doesn't think like this.

I have actually thought long and hard about my personal situation, and I have asked myself what I would do if one of those people killed by McVeigh were my kid, for example. And this is how Conservatives often frame the argument. Remember former presidential candidate Michael Dukakis being asked by Bernard Shaw if he would favor the death penalty if his wife was raped and murdered? Now, my answer is yes, I may be inclined to call for the death penalty, and I probably would fight for the death penalty, because I would be very angry and would want the perpetrator be punished to the fullest extent possible. But even though that is how I would *feel*, I would be wrong to fight for the death penalty. My point is that we are all emotional beings, and in instances when we are hurt we may feel compelled to reap vengeance, but it is the Government's job to do what is right, not what is emotional. Hence, the key question is what should be the public policy of the Government, a Government that is guided by Christian principles? Should the government satisfy the emotional appeal of its citizens and go against the teachings of Jesus, or should it go down the Christian path as set out by Jesus and refrain from executing people? I think it should be the latter. What do you think?

Now I want you to contrast O'Reilly's attitude above with the attitude of the Amish people whose children were murdered by Charles Roberts in Pennsylvania in October of 2006. Charles Roberts, a milk-truck driver who carried three guns and a childhood grudge, stormed the one-room Amish schoolhouse, sent the boys and adults outside, barricaded the doors with two-by-fours, and then opened fire on a dozen girls, killing two of them before committing suicide. Most of the victims were shot execution-style at point-blank range after being lined up along the chalkboard, their feet bound with wire and plastic ties. Three more girls died later making it a total of five who died. The parents of the girls and the Amish community ultimately forgave the killer, in a remarkable display of Christian love. They even met with Roberts' wife and other relatives of his. It was just incredibly remarkable the way the Amish people handled the situation, and I have no doubt in my mind that they are genuine Christians who follow the teachings of Jesus. I will always talk about this story, because I'm not sure I can forgive the way these people forgave. God bless them.

I ask you to contrast the Amish people's actions with O'Reilly's views because what you have here are two opposing beliefs. Now, these beliefs are so different that it is hard to argue that O'Reilly belongs to the same religion and share the same moral beliefs as the Amish people on this particular issue. I happen to believe that the Amish people's position is the Christian position and O'Reilly's position is the un-Christian position, because there is no way we can reconcile O'Reilly's position with the position of the Amish people, it's night and day. So again, I have to ask Conservatives for clarification on what they believe, and demand an explanation from them as to why they think those beliefs empower them to call themselves Christians.

Even more troubling is Conservatives' support for executing juveniles or people who were juveniles when they committed their crimes. Executing adults is one thing, but for people to have no reservations about executing children under eighteen, that's another thing. In March of 2005 a case went before the U.S. Supreme Court concerning a Missouri man who was seventeen when he killed a woman. The issue before the Supreme Court Justices was whether the death penalty should be applied if someone was a minor at the time when they committed the crime. The so-called Liberal judges, John Paul Stevens, David Souter, Ruth Bader Ginsberg, and Steven Breyer, along with Moderate Judge Anthony Kennedy, opposed the execution of juveniles. The Conservative judges, William Rehnquist, Antonin Scalia, Clarence Thomas, and Sandra Day O'Connor dissented and opined that it was okay to execute juveniles.

Now, I may be wrong, but I think all four of these Conservative Supreme Court Justices would describe themselves as Christians. But are they? Do these four Justices think that Jesus would have supported the execution of juveniles? Whether it is "legal" or not, shouldn't these Conservatives be guided by their Christian beliefs, rather than by legalisms and technical arguments? Legal arguments can be used to justify anything. There are good legal arguments on both sides of the issue, so in that sense the issue cannot be resolved by legal arguments alone. At the end of the day, on an issue like the death penalty, it is our moral conviction that is the final arbiter of our legal position. So I actually believe that an issue such as the death penalty, particularly the death penalty for juveniles, is not really a legal issue, and those charged with making decisions about it inevitably have to let their conscience have the final say. My final analysis tells me that the consciences of Justices Rehnquist, Scalia, Thomas, and O'Conner tell them that it is okay to execute juveniles, while the consciences of Justices Stevens, Souter, Ginsberg, Bryer, and Kennedy tell them that it is wrong to execute juveniles. I believe that the latter group of Justices has taken the Christian position, and the former has taken the unchristian position.

4) Public display of religiousness

Here again, Conservatives are way off base and counter to what Jesus taught. Conservatives seem to think that God will reward us based on how big a public display we make about our faith. I sometimes get the impression that these guys (and some gals like Ann Coulter and Michelle Malkin) have never read Jesus' teachings on the subject, so let me lay it out loud and clear. Here is what Jesus had to say about public display of religiousness:

> "And when you pray, you must not be like the hypocrites; for they love to stand and pray in the synagogues and at the street corners, that they might be seen by men. Truly I say to you, they have received their reward. But when you pray, go into your room and shut the door and pray to your Father who sees in secret and will reward you."[7]

Wow. Are Conservatives listening to this? Boy, how relevant this passage is to today's debate regarding the public display of religion and faith. Jesus more or less says to your face that you are a hypocrite if you pray in public for people to see. He says that prayer is private, God hears us when we pray in private, and it's not necessary to pray in public for other people to see. In essence, Prayer is not about showing other people how rich your faith is; prayer is a private conversation with God.

The above admonishment from Jesus makes perfect sense, doesn't it? Think of it: If you believe that God is an all-powerful God, hearing everything, knowing everything, seeing everything, and so on, he will hear your prayers wherever you are. Being in private doesn't hinder your communication with God, so why would you want to show the public that you're praying, or prove to the public that your faith in God is strong? It doesn't matter what other people believe about you, what matters is what you have in your heart and what God sees coming out of you.

The key question is whether someone's public display of faith and religion bears any relationship to his or her goodness as a human being, or his or her commitment to Christian principles. Does public display of faith and religion by an individual necessarily mean that that individual is a morally upright person? And conversely, can an individual who keeps his or her faith and religion to himself or herself be a morally upright person? Clearly, the above passage tells us that public display of faith and religion is not necessary, and it even suggests that those who engage in public displays of faith and religion are hypocrites. Do some names come to mind?

Why then do Conservatives insist on talking publicly about their faith, and fight for public displays of Christianity, when Jesus clearly taught that this is not necessary and might even be hypocritical? I can think of three reasons:

i) Being a real Christian is hard. It is hard to share what you have with the poor, it is hard to forgive people, it is hard to humble yourself and see the other person's point of view, it is hard to seek peace when the other side is belligerent, and so on. So the next best thing is to *appear* to be a Christian. Hence, we have phonies like Bill O'Reilly and other Conservatives running around and pretending to be Christians, when in fact they are far removed from Jesus' teachings.

ii) People like Bill O'Reilly, Jerry Falwell, Pat Robertson, and other conservative leaders use Christianity to promote themselves and develop a following among the masses. So they use these emotional issues (like placing the ten commandments in public places, reading the Bible in schools, saying "Merry Christmas" instead of "Happy Holidays", etc.) to drum up religious fervor among their followers to strengthen their position as a "leader". Now this is not something unique to Conservative Christians, it happens everywhere, but I'm just dealing here with Christianity so that's why I'm singling out these Conservatives.

iii) Conservatives either do not know the teachings of Jesus or think that it is not important to follow Jesus' teachings for whatever reason. I happen to think this does play a large part in the equation, because when I listen to Conservative Christian preachers (and Conservatives commentators & politicians) they do not talk about Luke 18:24, or Luke 16:19, or Matthew 25:31, or Matthew 5:39, or Matthew 6:5. They love to dwell on other issues that serve their personal interest rather than the interest of Christianity.

5) Universal Humanity

Conservatives often mock and criticize people (Americans) who show feelings of empathy or compassion towards the peoples of other countries. Such Americans are branded "haters" of America, or are sarcastically labeled "internationalists". Sometimes, if the United States of America does something that negatively affects people in other countries, and you empathize with those people and say you don't agree with what the United States did, you are labeled "unpatriotic" or "un-American". Now, the thing I don't understand is this: what part of the Christian ethics says that it is okay to discriminate between human beings because they are from a different country? I would like someone to show me where in the Gospel does it say that you are supposed to put the interest of your particular country above the interest of Humanity as a whole. In fact, the Gospel teaches us to do quite the opposite. Jesus never taught us to be parochial in our compassion. We are supposed to view all human beings the same, regardless of which country they live in. Based on my understanding of Jesus' teachings, an American is no more precious than a non-American, and we are not supposed to turn a blind eye to suffering people in other countries, or ignore their point of view simply because they are not Americans. Do Conservatives think that God cares who is an American and who is not? Do Conservatives believe that God loves Americans more than other nationalities? If they do, then they are definitely missing the main point of Christianity.

Jesus' teaching about helping people is clear: we are not supposed to help, or refuse to help, because someone is, or isn't, from our "group". So this really isn't just about nationality, it really is about race, color, religion, nationality, etc. etc. Jesus taught us that our "neighbor" is really *anybody*, even our enemies. Many of you I'm sure may know the parable of the Good Samaritan, found in Luke 10: 25. Here a lawyer gets up and asks Jesus what he (the lawyer) should do to inherit eternal life. Jesus answered him by asking him what is written in the Bible about this subject. He replied by saying that "Thou shalt love the Lord thy God with all thy heart, and with all thy soul, and with all they strength, and with all thy mind; and thy neighbor as thyself."[8] Jesus then told him to go and do just that. But the lawyer wanted to test Jesus further, so he pressed on and asked Jesus what exactly does he mean by *neighbor*, or who exactly is his neighbor. Jesus then explained the concept of "neighbor" by telling a parable, and here is where the story becomes very important to us as Christians. In the parable (Luke 10:25), as told by Jesus, a man was traveling from Jerusalem to Jericho, and he was robbed and beaten by thieves and left for dead. A priest came walking down the road where the man's body lay, but went over to the other side of the street as soon as he spotted the body. A Levite also passed by but didn't help the man. Finally, a Samaritan riding a beast was passing by, and he stopped to render assistance to the wounded man. The Samaritan bound up the wounds of the man, put him on his beast and took him to an inn. He paid the innkeeper some money and told the innkeeper that if it costs more he will pay him the balance when be comes back. Jesus then asked the lawyer which of the three of these people was the neighbor to the wounded man, and the lawyer answered that the Samaritan was the neighbor. Jesus then told the lawyer to go and follow that example.

The other extremely important aspect to the parable is the fact that Jesus chose a *Samaritan* to be the good neighbor as an example. The reason he did this was because Samaritans and Jews did not like each other, and Jesus wanted to point out that even though the Samaritan was passing through a Jewish neighborhood and saw that it was a Jew who was wounded and needed help, he did not walk away, he helped someone who was more or less an enemy. So this idea we often hear from Conservative that your country comes first is actually un-Christian, based on Jesus' teachings. Patriotism is not a concept to be found in Christianity. Now I'm not saying it is wrong to be patriotic, and I am not encouraging people to be unpatriotic. What I'm saying is that if you boast that you are a *Christian*, patriotism should not be one of the things that rank high as a priority, because Jesus taught us to love all people. We are all God's children, and country should not be a barrier to our love and kindness.

So in summary, this is my overall interpretation of what it means to be a Christian, based on the true definition of the word, and the teachings of Jesus, as I understand them. My concept of a Christian is vastly different from that of Bill O'Reilly and other Conservatives. In fact, my understanding of what it means to be a Christian is antithetical in many ways to what Conservatives like Bill O'Reilly and others believe. This being the case, I don't think we belong to the same religion or worship the same God. I believe that Conservatives have perverted Christianity by suppressing the teachings of Jesus and replacing it with their own twisted political ideology. It is time for those of us who truly believe in the teachings of Jesus to stand up and argue our case forcefully. We must not back away when Conservatives raise the topic of religion. I believe that we are on the right side, and Conservatives are on the wrong side. If we stick to the arguments I outlined in this chapter, we will always win the debate. We have to stop playing defense, and start playing offense.

Footnotes to Chapter Four

1) Luke 18: 24-25

2) Luke 16: 19-25

3) Matthew 25: 31-46

4) Matthew 5: 38-45

5) Matthew 5: 21

6) WorldNetDaily, June 14, 2001

7) Matthew 6: 5-7

8) Luke 10: 27

5

The ACLU And Religion In America

One of the worst cases of propaganda spewing from Bill O'Reilly has been his dishonest reporting on the ACLU. He has misrepresented the objectives and the intentions of the ACLU, and has attempted to tarnish the organization's image, simply because the ACLU opposes the Bush Administration on some Civil Liberty issues and is against some other Conservative causes. Particularly offensive has been O'Reilly's reporting in the area of religion, claiming that the ACLU wants to remove religion from the American society, and that they are seeking to promote a secular agenda. In his own words:

> "The American Civil Liberties Union, along with legal secularists like Supreme Court justices Ruth Bader Ginsberg and John Paul Stevens, are using the Constitution to bludgeon any form of public spirituality."[1]

Bludgeon any form of public spirituality? What is O'Reilly talking about? Perhaps he should read the case of the ACLU helping Rev. Todd Pyle in Virginia to conduct baptisms in the public parks. Or the case of Westfield High School in Massachusetts, where the ACLU fought against the school's ban on distributing candy canes with religious message. The ACLU has always stood up and fought for people's religious rights. The public record is replete with public statements and court cases that demonstrate the ACLU's commitment to freedom of religion in the United States. The purpose of this chapter is to highlight some of these statements and cases so you can see for yourself that the ACLU is not an anti-spiritual or anti-religious organization as O'Reilly claims. It's quite the opposite. The ACLU believes in religious freedom and has consistently fought for these rights.

O'Reilly engages in the classic propaganda techniques of *Misrepresentation* and *Omission* whenever he reports on the ACLU. First he confuses, deliberately I think, private religious expression with public or government sponsored religious expression. The ACLU firmly supports private religious expression, but opposes government sponsored religious expression, because they think it is unconstitutional. The ACLU believes in the concept of *Separation of Church and State*, an issue I deal with extensively in Chapter Six. Basically, the ACLU believes that the Government should stay out of religion and let private citizens be free to practice their religion as they see fit, within the confines of the laws. O'Reilly misleads his audience by conflating the two concepts. He fails to make the distinction between private religious expression and government sponsored religious expression, and instead lumps the two issues together as one. He then proceeds to cherry pick a few cases where the ACLU opposed *government sponsored* religious expression and presents them as evidence that the ACLU is anti-religious. This is *Misrepresentation.* To compound this, he completely leaves out the cases that the ACLU took on that support private religious expression. He did not even mention one of them. Here he engages in *Omission.* It is now my job to tell you about these cases so that you can decide for yourself whether you think the ACLU is against religion in America, as O'Reilly constantly asserts.

Here are ten cases in which the ACLU stood up for the religious rights of ordinary people. You would not hear about these cases on *The O'Reilly Factor*, because they do not comport with O'Reilly's agenda.

1) ACLU of Virginia threatened to file a lawsuit against Virginia officials for imposing a ban against Baptism in Public Parks

On Sunday May 23, 2004 Rev. Todd Pyle of the Cornerstone Baptist Church had planned to conduct a series of baptisms in Falmouth Waterside Park in Stafford County, but was advised by Brian Robinson, the Park Manager, that religious activities were not allowed in the park. The ACLU of Virginia immediately informed Rev. Pyle that he had a constitutional right to conduct baptisms in the park and threatened to challenge in federal court the Park Authority's ban on religious activities. The Federicksburg-Stafford Park Authority, which controlled access to the public park, backed off and announced that it would issue written policies making it clear that religious groups have the same right to use the park as all other groups. For the record, here is what Kent Willis, Executive Director ACLU of Virginia said about the matter: "The rules are really very simple, Government officials merely need to make sure that religious activities have the same rights as any other activities in a public park. If swimming is allowed, then baptism must be allowed. If groups can gather for sports or cultural activities, then groups can gather for religious ceremonies."

(Based on this first case alone, this doesn't sound like an anti-religious organization to me.)

2) ACLU of Massachusetts defended students punished for distributing candy canes with religious messages

In 2002, schools officials at Westfield High School in Western Massachusetts imposed a one-day suspension on a group of students for distributing candy canes with religious messages just before Christmas. The basis for the school's disciplinary action was a school rule that prohibited the distribution of all literature that is not related to the curriculum. The ACLU of Massachusetts sided with the students and filed legal papers in February of 2003 on their behalf, arguing that the school rule violated both state law and the First Amendment, which protected the students' speech as long as it did not disrupt the educational process. Here is what the ACLU cooperating attorney Jeffrey Pyle, the main author of the friend-of-the-court brief said at the time of the ACLU's action: "Students have a right to communicate ideas, religious or otherwise, to other students during their free time, before or after class, in the cafeteria, or elsewhere." (Incidentally, Jeffrey Pyle was a plaintiff in a landmark free speech/religion case back in 1996 when he was a high school senior—Pyle vs South Hadley School Committee. In that case Pyle was disciplined by Hadley School for wearing a T-shirt with religious message. He sued and won, and that case became a landmark case establishing a precedent for free speech and religion in school.)

(Are you convinced yet that O'Reilly has misrepresented the stance of the ACLU on religion?)

3) ACLU of Michigan defended the right of a Christian valedictorian to have a religious entry in the school's yearbook

In 2001, Abbey Moler, a devout Christian, submitted the following Bible verse as an entry for the 2001 yearbook at Stevenson High School in Sterling Heights which she attended:
"'For I know the plans I have for you,' declares the Lord, 'plans to prosper you and not to harm you, plans to give you hope and a future.' Jeremiah 29:11 (New International Bible)."
    When the yearbook was published, however, Moler discovered that her entry was omitted. She and her parents complained, and were told that the school

could not publish the entry due to its religious content. The ACLU of Michigan took up Moler's case and reached an out of court settlement with the school authorities, Utica Community School District, which included the following:

—The district placed a sticker with Moler's original entry in the copies of the yearbook on file with the school;

—The district instructed the Stevenson High School yearbook staff not to censor students' yearbook entries solely because they contain religious or political speech that others might find offensive;

—The district provided and will continue to provide in-service training and advice to school staff on free speech and religious freedom issues that arise in school;

—The district wrote a letter of regret to Moler apologizing for the failure to include her entry in the yearbook.

Here is what the Legal Director of ACLU Michigan Michael J. Steinberg said about the case:

"While it is true that the Constitution forbids public schools to promote religion, schools must be careful not to suppress the private religious expression of students. In this case, a high school purported to create an open forum for student expression, yet censored a student's speech because it was religious in nature."

(It's just unbelievable that O'Reilly has been allowed to tarnish the ACLU they way he did, isn't it?)

4) ACLU supported the right of Iowa students to distribute Christian literature at school

In July of 2002 the Iowa Civil Liberties Union publicly announced that it was supporting a group of Christian students who had filed a lawsuit against Davenport schools to fight for the right to distribute religious literature during non-instructional time. The case was brought by Davenport students Sasha Dean, Jaron Dean, and Becky Swope, and was filed in Federal Court on May 31, 2002. This is a clear indication not only that the ACLU is not anti-religious, but also that it strongly supports the right of religious people to exercise their fundamental rights. Here is what Executive Director of the ICLU Ben Stone said at the time:

"The school's policy against the distribution of religious literature outside of class is clearly wrong. Not only does the policy violate the students' right to freely exercise their religious beliefs, but it also infringes on their free speech rights."

(Is this the same ACLU that O'Reilly says is a "secular" organization?)

5) ACLU of New Jersey joined in lawsuit supporting a Second Grader's right to sing "Awesome God" at talent show

In a free speech case, Turton, et al. v. Frenchtown Elementary School, et al., filed in Federal Court in 2005 in Trenton, New Jersey, the ACLU supported the right of a Second Grade student, Olivia Turton, to sing the song "Awesome God" at a voluntary after school talent show. School officials had banned the student from singing the song on the grounds that it was promoting religion in the school. But the ACLU disagreed, and argued that the student had the right to sing "Awesome God", since the talent show was a voluntary after school affair and the school had left the choice of song up to the individual students as long as the songs were "G-rated". The ACLU cooperating attorney had this to say:
"There is distinction between speech by a school and speech by individual students. The Constitution protects a student's individual right to express herself, including the right to express herself religiously."

(What more evidence do you need to prove that O'Reilly is a propagandist?)

6) ACLU helped free New Mexico street preacher from prison

In 2005, the ACLU of New Mexico took up the case of a street preacher who was arrested by Portales police. The police claimed that the street preacher, Shawn Miller, was "yelling" at passing cars. The ACLU became involved after Miller's wife sent a letter requesting assistance. She said that she and her two children had been with Miller on April 17 when he was arrested by Portales police for "disorderly conduct". Miller had been preaching in a lot of an abandoned gas station that is commonly used by street vendors. The ACLU managed to get him released on bond, and here is what the Executive Director of ACLU New Mexico said about the case:
"Mr. Miller has a guaranteed right to stand on a street corner and proclaim his faith in God to all who pass by. He wasn't harassing or intimidating anyone. He certainly should not have spent time under lock and key for such a minor incident."

Incidentally, this case was also supported by the Conservative organization The American Family Association, which collaborated with the ACLU throughout the case. So what we had here was the ACLU working closely with a Christian Conservative group in the interest of freedom of religion. How then can O'Reilly argue that the ACLU is a secular organization?

(What say you, Bill O'Reilly? You may want to rethink your position, Sir)

7) ACLU of Nebraska defended church faced with eviction by the City of Lincoln

In 2004, the City of Lincoln threatened to shut down and evict a Presbyterian Church (The Church of the Awesome God) because the church was located at the edge of an area zoned for industrial use. The city was requesting that the church hire a mechanical engineer and install a new air intake system with shut-off valve in case of a hazardous spill, something which the small congregation could not afford to do. The ACLU stepped in and argued that the city was treating the church differently from other establishments. It noted that no other businesses in the industrial zones were required to have that sort of expensive renovation. Here is what the Legal Director of ACLU Nebraska, Amy Miller, said:

"The First Amendment guarantees the right to free exercise of religion. A church cannot be forced to close its doors unless the city can prove there is a compelling reason to shut them down. In this case, the church is a small congregation that causes no problems for anyone. The city has failed to provide a single reason for ordering our client out...."

There are two more cases worth noting, where the ACLU has intervened on behalf of churches that were denied zoning permits by local authorities. First, there is the case of *Second Baptist Church of Homestead v. Borough of West Mifflin*. In this case, the ACLU of Greater Pittsburgh took up the case of the Second Baptist Church of Homestead after the Borough of West Mifflin in Pennsylvania refused to issue an occupancy permit for an abandoned church building that the Church has purchased. The ACLU won the case and the Borough ended up issuing the permit. Then, there is *Tabernacle Community Baptist Church v. City of East Point*. In this case the City of East Point in Georgia denied the Tabernacle Community Baptist Church a zoning permit to establish its house of worship in a building they were planning to purchase. The City of East Point's action was based on a local ordinance that prohibited churches from occupying structures that had previously been used for commercial purposes. Because the ordinance allowed a secular entity to purchase the building but not a religious group, The ACLU of Georgia filed a lawsuit against the City of East Point in April 2006 claiming that the ordinance violated the United States and Georgia Constitutions. The ACLU asked the court to overturn the ordinance and allow the church to establish a place of worship on the property in question.

(How can you call an organization that is helping to keep churches open a secular organization?)

8) ACLU of New Jersey successfully defends right of religious expression by jurors

In 2003, prosecutors in a criminal case in New Jersey Superior Court in Essex County dismissed two jurors on the grounds that they (the jurors) were "demonstrative about their religion" and that such persons "tend to favor defendants". One juror was dismissed for wearing a particular religious clothing, and the other for having engaged in missionary activity. The ACLU of New Jersey filed a friend-of-the-court brief arguing that the prosecutor's action violated the equal protection and freedom of religion clauses of the United States and New Jersey Constitutions, as well as the right to a trial by an impartial Jury. The New Jersey Supreme Court sided with the ACLU of New Jersey. The Legal Director of ACLU of New Jersey Ed Barocas said:
"In this country, people have a right to express their religious beliefs without fear of discrimination by the government. Excluding people from jury pools based on their religious belief or expression violates the principles of freedom found in the Bill of Rights."

(Bill O'Reilly either does know what he is talking about or he is just deliberately misleading the public.)

9) ACLU of Rhode Island filed appeal on behalf of a Christian prisoner barred from preaching at religious services

In 2006 the ACLU of Rhode Island took up the case of Wesley Spratt, a Christian prisoner in the Adult Correctional Facility in Rhode Island, who was barred from preaching in 2003 by prison officials on "security" grounds. Sprat had been preaching in the facility for seven years until a new warden took over in 2003 and decided that it was not safe to allow Spratt to continue preaching. A lower court (U.S. Magistrate Jacob Hagopian) had actually upheld the ban, but the ACLU appealed the case on behalf of Spratt and argued that Spratt's right to preach and practice his religion was protected by a Federal Law known as RLUIPA. RLUIPA is a statute that was drafted to protect the religious freedom of people who are institutionalized. The ACLU sought a court order to allow Spratt to continue preaching at religious services.

(You have to be a lunatic to call an organization that is fighting for the religious rights of prisoners a secular organization.)

10) The ACLU teamed up with Rev. Jerry Falwell against a provision in the Virginia Constitution that banned religious organizations from incorporating

In this case, the ACLU of Virginia joined with the Rev. Jerry Falwell in 2002 in a lawsuit against the State of Virginia for prohibiting Churches from incorporating. The prohibition was based on the 18th Century Virginia Constitution that prohibited religious institutions from incorporating. The ACLU joined the lawsuit as a "friend of the court" and challenged the ban on the grounds that it violates the U.S. Constitution's guarantee of free exercise of religion. The judge agreed with the Rev. Jerry Falwell and the ACLU, and struck down the ban, ruling that religious institutions must be allowed to incorporate. The Executive Director of ACLU Virginia Kent Willis had this to say about the case:

"Virginia's 18th century lawmakers had good intentions when they decided not to allow churches to incorporate. At that time only the General Assembly had the power to grant corporate status, and the framers of the Constitution did not want a political body deciding which religious institutions would be allowed to incorporate and which ones would not. That would hardly be a good start for the still novel idea of religious freedom. But that was long before the modern concept of incorporation, which is an administrative rather than political process. The old law, placed in the modern context, discriminates against religious institutions by denying them the same opportunity to incorporate as other similar institutions."

(Why would the ACLU team up with Jerry Falwell and fight for the right of churches in VA to incorporate if they were an anti-religious group, Mr. O'Reilly?)

So having read these ten cases, do you still think that O'Reilly is right when he says that the ACLU wants to remove religion from our society? He can't possibly be right, because if the ACLU were anti-religious it would not have taken up the cases above. In fact, the above cases prove that the ACLU *favors* people's religious rights; they are not even a *neutral* organization, they *support* people's religious rights. So O'Reilly's charges against the ACLU are totally without merit. I believe these charges are a deliberate attempt to discredit the ACLU, because the ACLU opposes government involvement with religion. O'Reilly favors bringing religion into the public and into Government, and because the ACLU believes in the separation of church and state, O'Reilly wants to demonize them. But the ACLU is on the right side of the separation of church and state issue. The founding fathers Thomas Jefferson and James Madison firmly believed in the separation of church and state, and wanted to keep religion out of Government, as I argue in the next Chapter.

Footnotes to Chapter Five:

1) Who's Looking Out for You, Bill O'Reilly, page 113.

6

Separation Of Church And State

"To any intellectually honest person, it is apparent that the Founders wanted very much to keep God in the public arena, even uppermost in the thoughts of the populace."[1]

The above quote from Bill O'Reilly raises two questions: One, did the Founding Fathers want the government to keep God and religion in the public arena? And two, did they propose a way to keep God and religion in the public arena? Bill O'Reilly does what all Conservatives do whenever the topic of Church and State comes up: they quote the Founding Fathers' statements on their *personal* religious beliefs and say that that is proof that the Founding Fathers wanted the *government* to somehow support religion. Here is the evidence O'Reilly has to offer on the issue:

"In 1781, Jefferson said the following words, which are engraved on the Jefferson Memorial in Washington: 'God who gave us life gave us liberty. Can the liberties of a nation be secured when we have removed a conviction that these liberties are the gift of God?"[2]

"Said Madison: 'We have staked the whole future of American civilization, not upon the power of government, far from it. We have staked the future of all of our political institutions upon the capacity of mankind for self-government; upon the capacity of each and all of us to govern ourselves, to control ourselves, to sustain ourselves according to The Ten Commandments'."[3]

"In 1787, Franklin delivered a stirring speech at the Constitutional Convention in which he said: 'I therefore beg leave to move—that henceforth, prayers imploring the assistance of Heaven and its blessings on our deliberations, be held in this Assembly every morning before we proceed to business, and that one or more of the clergy of this city be requested to officiate in that service'."[4]

But there is *nothing* in these three quotes that shows that Jefferson, Madison, or Franklin, believed that the *government* should support religion. The argument from right-wing Conservatives seems to be that because the Founding Fathers were religious men, it logically follows that they favored government involvement in religion. But they cannot provide any quote from these great men showing that they advocated government support for religion. It is one thing to be religious, but it is another thing to be in favor of government support of religion. The above quotes in no way, shape, or form, show that the Founding Fathers wanted the government to support religion. Is it logical then to conclude that because the Founding Fathers themselves were religious, they favored government support of religion? The answer is no, for two reasons: Firstly, I can equally produce statements from these great men to show their hostility and skepticism towards religion and government involvement in religion:

"History I believe furnishes no example of a priest-ridden people maintaining a free civil government. This marks the lowest grade of ignorance, of which their political as well as religious leaders will avail themselves for their own purpose."[5]

"The settled opinion here is that religion is essentially distinct from Civil Govt. and exempt from its cognizance; that a connexion between them is injurious to both; that there are causes in the human breast which ensure the perpetuity of religion without the aid of the law...."[6]

"When a religion is good, I conceive that it will support itself; and, when it cannot support itself, and God does not take care to support, so that its Professors are obliged to call for the help of the Civil Power, it is a sign, I apprehend, of its being a bad one."[7]

So if O'Reilly and his Conservative friends want to play the quotation game we can do that all day long, and for every quote they produce to support their argument I can produce a better one to counter. Actually, the three quotes I laid out above do by themselves make a good case that these three men did not favor the government getting involved with religion. But this issue should not be examined and resolved solely by the use of quotes, even though my counter quotes above clearly show that Jefferson, Franklin, and Madison did believe that religion should be kept out of government. We have to delve into the history of the founding of the Republic, and go back to the early days to find out what the Founding Fathers' public policy positions were as it specifically pertains to *government support for religion*. That brings me to my second point, which is, that the historical evidence prove that the Founding Fathers did in fact firmly believe in the separation of church and state.

Let's start with the United States Constitution, because this is the supreme document that the Founding Fathers framed to govern the land. Bill O'Reilly and religious Conservatives love to go back to other documents, like the Northwest Ordinance, for example. But who cares about the Northwest Ordinance? How many of you have ever heard of the Northwest Ordinance, by the way? I never heard about it until I read about it in O'Reilly's criticism of the Supreme Court justices who support separation of church and state:

> "... And those jurists must really hate 1787, because also in that year the Northwest Ordinance was passed to govern the territories not yet admitted into the Union. Article III of that ordinance states: 'Religion, morality, and knowledge being necessary to good government and the happiness of mankind, schools, and the means of education shall be forever encouraged.'"[8]

Well, Mr. O'Reilly, we are not governed by the Northwest Ordinance today, and so it is totally irrelevant to the discussion at hand. The Supreme Court justices didn't swear to uphold the Northwest Ordinances, they swore to uphold the United States Constitution, which says: "Congress shall make no laws respecting an establishment of religion". The Founding Fathers set up a Constitution, and the Constitution trumps all other documents, including the Declaration of Independence, by the way. My question therefore to Bill O'Reilly and other Conservatives is this: If the Founding Fathers so strongly believed that government should support religion, as you claim, why did they not include that in the Constitution? **The Founding Fathers had a chance to put God and Religion in the Constitution, but they chose not to**.

The right-wing ideologues cannot put forth any *evidence* that the Founding Fathers wanted government to support religion, because there is none, so they muddy the issue by bringing in statements made by these great men concerning their *personal* religious beliefs and use that as the basis for saying that the Founding Fathers were against the separation of Church and State. But we have two separate and distinct issues here: one is the Founding Fathers' personal religious beliefs, and the other is whether or not they were in favor of the government supporting religion. So again, let's not confuse the issues. No one is arguing that the

Founding Fathers weren't religious, that's not the issue. We all agree that they believed in God. The issue is whether they were in favor of the government getting involved with religious issues or wanted the government to support religion in any way.

Conservatives have to understand that a political leader can be religious but at the same he or she could also believe that government should *not* get involved in religious matters. That doesn't mean that the political leader in question is unreligious, or that his or her position is morally inconsistent. It just means that they don't want the government to meddle with religion. Former President Jimmy Carter is a modern day example of one such people. He is a devout Christian, but he firmly believes in the separation of church and state. So having a personal belief in God does not *necessarily* mean that one supports religion in public or government involvement in religion. And in fact, this was the position of the prominent Founding Fathers—Jefferson, Madison, and Franklin. They were religious men, but they firmly believed that religion is *personal,* something between an individual and his God, and not something for the government to get involved with. Remember that the Founding Fathers had just come out of a struggle with the British partly over religious freedom, so why would they want to go back to a system of religious tyranny where the government supported religion? It doesn't make sense. The Founding Fathers were too wise to let their religious sentiments take them down that slippery slope.

Thomas Jefferson

In 1779 Jefferson wrote a bill called a Bill for Establishing Religious Freedom, and in the preamble he argued as follows:

> "… our civil rights have no dependence on our religious opinions, any more than our opinions in physics or geometry; that therefore the proscribing any citizen as unworthy the public confidence by laying upon him an incapacity of being called to offices of trust and emolument, unless he profess or renounce this or that religious opinion, is depriving him injuriously of those privileges and advantages to which, in common with his fellow citizens, he has a natural right…."[9]

Does this sound like a man who favored bringing religion into government?

When be became president, Thomas Jefferson made popular the phrase "wall of separation between church and state". O'Reilly says that "Letters written by these great men show that they believed social stability could be achieved only by a people who embraced a moral God"[10], but he fails to tell you about one important letter written by Jefferson that expresses Jefferson's view of church and state. On October 7, 1801, the Danbury Baptist Association of Connecticut wrote to Jefferson, partly to congratulate him on his ascendancy to the Presidency, but partly to also express concern with the Church-State relationship in Connecticut. On January 1, 1802 Jefferson wrote back to the Danbury Baptist Association and explained his position on church and state. Below is the full text of the letter:

> To Mess. Nehemia Dodge, Ephraim Robbins, & Stephen S. Nelson, a committee of the Danbury Baptist association in the state of Connecticut.
> Gentlemen
> The affectionate sentiments of esteem and approbation which you are so good as to express towards me, on behalf of the Danbury Baptist association, give me the highest satisfaction, my duties dictate a faithful & zealous pursuit of the interest of my constituents, & in proportion as they are persuaded of my fidelity to those duties, the discharge of them becomes more and more pleasing.
> Believing with you that religion is a matter which lies solely between Man & his God, that he owes account to none other for his faith or his worship, that the legitimate powers of government reach actions only, & not opinions, I contemplate with sovereign reverence that act of the whole American people which declared that their legislature should 'make no law respecting an establishment of religion, or prohibiting the free exercise thereof,' thus building a wall of separation between Church & State. Adhering to this expression of the supreme will of the nation in behalf of the rights of conscience, I shall see with sincere satisfaction the progress of those sentiments which tend to restore to man all his natural rights, convinced he has no natural right in opposition to his social duties.
>
> I reciprocate your kind prayers for the protection & blessing of the common father and creator of man, and tender you for yourselves and your religious association, assurances of my high respect & esteem.
>
> Th. Jefferson
>
> Jan 1, 1802.

So there you have it. It couldn't be clearer. Jefferson says that by declaring that congress shall make no law concerning the establishment or prohibition of religion, the constitution has effectively built a wall of separation between Church and State. This is what Jefferson says, I'm not making this up. So when O'Reilly and the American right-wing tell you that the Founding Fathers favored government getting involved with religion they are clearly misguided. But Jefferson's letter to the Danbury Baptists doesn't end here. The letter above is the *final* version of Jefferson's letter. Jefferson's *original* version was much stronger in it's support for separation of Church and State. The original draft had sections of it penned out in ink and for years no one knew what Jefferson has penned out, but thanks to Louis Freeh who permitted the FBI Laboratory to apply its state-of-the-art technology to the task of restoring Jefferson's obliterated words, we now know the exact text of Jefferson's original unedited draft. Here it is:

To Mess. Nehemia Dodge, Ephraim Robbins, & Stephen S. Nelson, a committee of the Danbury Baptist association in the state of Connecticut.
Gentlemen
The affectionate sentiments of esteem and approbation which you are so good as to express towards me, on behalf of the Danbury Baptist association, give me the highest satisfaction, my duties dictate a faithful & zealous pursuit of the interest of my constituents, & in proportion as they are persuaded of my fidelity to those duties, the discharge of them becomes more and more pleasing.
Believing with you that religion is a matter which lies solely between Man & his God, that he owes account to none other for his faith or his worship, that the legitimate powers of government reach actions only, & not opinions, I contemplate with sovereign reverence that act of the whole American people which declared that their legislature should 'make no law respecting an establishment of religion, or prohibiting the free exercise thereof,' thus building a wall of <u>eternal</u> separation between Church & State. Congress thus inhibited from acts respecting religion, and the Executive authorized only to execute their acts, I have refrained from prescribing even those occasional performances of devotion, practiced indeed by the Executive of another nation as the legal head of it's church, but subject here, as religious exercises only to the voluntary regulations and discipline of each respective sect. Confining myself therefore to the duties of my station, which are merely <u>temporal</u>, be assured that your religious rights shall never be infringed by any act of mine and that adhering to this expression of the supreme will of the nation in behalf of the rights of conscience, I shall see with friendly dispositions the progress of those sentiments which tend to restore to man all his natural rights, convinced he has no natural right in opposition to his social duties.
I reciprocate your kind prayers for the protection & blessing of the common father and creator of man, and tender you for yourselves & the Danbury Baptist association assurances of my high respect & esteem.
Th. Jefferson
Jan 1, 1802.

I underlined the words "eternal" and "temporal" because they further strengthen the already strong argument that Jefferson did not believe that government should be involved in religious matters. The use of these two words by Jefferson is devastating to religious Conservatives who want their politicians involved in religion. Jefferson wrote them with his own hands, which indicate that they came directly from his heart. The dictionary defines "eternal" as *having infinite duration; everlasting; continued without intermission; perpetual.*

This is pretty strong language from Jefferson, and one way to interpret the use of the word "eternal" is that Jefferson believed that this separation between Church and State must *never* be breached, regardless of the times or the situation. The use of the word "temporal" is even more devastating. It's explosive. The dictionary defines "temporal" as *of or relating to time as opposed to eternity; of or relating to earthly life; lay or secular rather than clerical or sacred; civil.*

Secular? Civil? Wow, this is bound to upset people like the Reverend Jerry Falwell and the Reverend Pat Robertson, don't you think? Jefferson saying that the duties of his station are secular, or civil? A president of the United States saying he has no religious role? They and their Conservative friends will try to spin this and say it doesn't mean what it says. But spinning this will be very difficult, because the words speak for themselves. Back then the word "temporal" was also closely associated with the British House of Lords, where you had lay members who were referred to as the "Lords Temporal" as opposed to the ecclesiastical members who were referred to as the "Lords Spiritual". So clearly Jefferson's use of the word "temporal" strongly suggests that he did not see his role as President of the United States as being one in which he should have anything to do with religion. He did not see himself as a religious or spiritual leader of any kind.

Think of it: Why would Jefferson in the first place even think of using these words in his original draft if he firmly believed that government *should* be involved in religious affairs, as the right-wing wants to have you believe? This was Jefferson writing from his heart, unedited. One should infer from it that this was the true expression of his opinion on the subject of church and state. Apparently, the reason why Jefferson altered his original draft was because he had passed the letter on to his then Attorney General Levy Lincoln for review, and Lincoln advised him against using some of the original language for fear of angering religious leaders. Jefferson heeded Lincoln's advice, and hence we have the final draft. So when O'Reilly proclaims that "One of the biggest fraud ever foisted upon the America people is the issue of separation of Church and State ...", his assertion looks foolish when you stack it up against Jefferson's own writings in this particular letter. There is no fraud. Based on Jefferson's writings, which you will see more of shortly, it is clear that he did not believe that it was a good idea to mix religion and politics. He did not believe that the government and its officials should take sides in any religious issue.

In fact, the U.S. Supreme Court has upheld the separation of church and state doctrine on more than one occasion. As early as 1878 in the case of Reynolds v. United States, the Supreme Court spotlighted the "wall of separation" phrase, saying that "it may be accepted almost as an authoritative declaration of the scope and effect of the first amendment". In 1947, the Everson case emerged as the first judicial guideline for the effective separation of church and state. That case concerned a New Jersey Board of Education that provided financial assistance for bus transportation to parents who were sending their children to and from Roman Catholic schools. The high court ruling that struck down that practice noted the following:

> "The 'establishment of religion' clause of the First Amendment means at least this: Neither a state nor the Federal Government can set up a church. Neither can pass laws which aid one religion, aid all religions, or prefer one religion over another.... Neither a state nor the Federal Government can, openly or secretly, participate in the affairs of any religious organizations or groups and vice versa. In the words of Jefferson, the clause against establishment of religion by law was intended to erect a 'wall of separation between Church and State.'"

You may notice that the last quote "a wall of separation between Church and State" is from Jefferson's 1802 letter to the Danbury Baptists that I dealt with earlier. But you might be surprised that Jefferson's letter to the Danbury Baptists is not the only piece of writing from Jefferson in which he expressed support for separation of church and state. Later, in 1817 Jefferson authored the Elementary School Act, in which he clearly stated that religion and religious teachings must be kept out of the public schools, and he specifically said that Ministers of Gospel should not visit public schools:

> "No religious reading, instruction or exercise, shall be prescribed or practiced in the elementary schools inconsistent with the tenets of any religious sect or denomination."[11]

> "Ministers of the Gospel are excluded from serving as Visitors to the county Elementary Schools to avoid jealously from other sects, were the public education committed to the ministers of a particular one; and with more reason

than in the case of their exclusion from the legislative and executive functions."[12]

It is clear that Jefferson did not want religion in the public schools. O'Reilly criticized Justice John Paul Stevens for opining that "School sponsorship of a religious message is impermissible."[13] And O'Reilly goes on to argue that "Yet a national poll on the situation found that two out of three Americans thought that the prayer should be permitted."[14] So I guess O'Reilly is now in favor of suspending the United States Constitution and governing the Republic by polls. Anyway, Justice Stevens is absolutely correct in rendering that opinion, and this is very much in line with Jefferson's way of thinking. Jefferson clearly saw the problem that multiple religions presented as it relates to the public school system. I guess religious Conservatives are so blinded by their piousness that they cannot see the bigger picture. My question to O'Reilly is, if he is saying that school sponsored religious message is okay in the public schools, then which religion should be allowed? Catholic? Presbyterian? Buddhism? Islam? (which interpretation?) Hinduism? (which sect?), Anglican? Baptist? Lutheran? All? If not all, then who should decide which one is to be allowed? Jefferson saw the practical problem with religion and public education and staked out a reasonable and tenable position; but ideologically driven Conservatives, like O'Reilly, remain in denial. The issue is quite simple: You cannot allow all religions in schools, that would lead to chaos, and so if you cannot allow all then you cannot allow any, because allowing particular ones means you are discriminating against the others. The logic is plain and simple; it has nothing to do with "anti-spiritual forces" as O'Reilly constantly claims.

O'Reilly goes on to say that: "In every debate about public spirituality, the secularists spin the issue and equate God with the legal concept of religion. The two are separate...."[15] This is one of the most absurd statements I have ever heard. It is utterly disingenuous to argue that you can separate *God* from *religion*. How? Exactly how do you teach someone about believing in God without teaching them about a particular religion, Mr. O'Reilly? As a practical matter, almost everyone who was taught about God from when he or she was a child was taught through a particular religion. So it's a bogus argument to say that somehow you can inform people about God without bringing in a particular religion. You cannot; it's impossible. How many people in America today believe in God but are not connected to a religious sect in one form or another in some way or another? The answer is none. Either their parents belonged to some sect, or their foreparents belonged to some sect, and the beliefs were passed down to them, and that's how they came to believe in God. There is no "generic" way to teach people about believing in God without bringing in religion; and there is no way you can "prove" the existence of God in the same way you can prove the existence of gravity. Religion is a matter of faith, so what you have to do is relate it to history, events, places, historical figures, etc., and this is where each sect comes in. Christians talk about Jesus, The Cross, Holy Communion, etc.; Muslims talk about Mohammed, Mecca, Ramadan, etc.; Hindus talk about Ram & Sita, Deepavali, Reincarnation, etc., etc. You get the idea. Added to this, each religion has its own set of holy books and its own set of principles and beliefs. If there were one generic way of teaching Godliness, the same way we teach Math or Physics, then we would have been one happy world. There would have been much less terrorism, much less bigotry, and much more love for each other. And, we wouldn't have needed religion, and we wouldn't be having this debate in the first place. Do you get it, O'Reilly? It's quite simple. So stop arguing that you can separate God from religion. You cannot.

The other important point to note regarding Jefferson's original draft to the Danbury Baptists is where he wrote "... I have refrained from prescribing even those occasional performances of devotion ...". Jefferson was referring to the fact that he broke with the tradition of George Washington and John Adams, first and second presidents respectively, who regularly proclaimed national days of fasting and thanksgiving. Jefferson stopped the practice, and as we shall see later James Madison (fourth president) continued Jefferson's practice with a few exceptions. Again, this is proof that Jefferson did not see himself as a religious or spiritual leader, nor did he think that the *government* should be involved in religious issues. Throughout Jefferson's eight years as president he refrained from making these religious proclamations. He took a tremendous amount of heat for his stance, particularly from New England Federalists. In fact, Jefferson was branded an atheist by some. Back in the presidential campaign of 1800, the Federalists had attacked Jefferson as an infidel, claiming that his "intoxication" with the religious and political extremism of the French Revolution disqualified him from public office. So clearly Jefferson was not a leader possessed with religious fervor, as Conservatives often claim. Jefferson was a pragmatist.

James Madison

O'Reilly picked one quote from Madison and claimed that it represents Madison's definitive opinion on the subject of separation of Church and State. But it is not true that Madison opposed the separation of Church and State, as O'Reilly wants you to believe. The fact is that Madison was a firm believer in the separation of Church and State. In 1786 he took up Jefferson's Bill for Establishing Religious Freedom that I mentioned above, and which had not yet become law, and pushed it through the Virginia legislature and got it passed into law. Many years later, in 1819, Madison wrote to his friend Robert Walsh, and reflected with pride on the passage of Jefferson's Bill for Establishing Religious Freedom:

> "It was the Universal opinion of the Century preceding the last that Civil Government could not stand without the prop of a Religious establishment, and that the Christian religion itself, would perish if not supported by the legal provision for its Clergy. The experience of Virginia conspicuously corroborates the disproof of both opinions. The civil Government, though bereft of every thing like an associated hierarchy, possesses the requisite stability, and performs its functions with complete success; whilst the number, the industry, and the morality of the Priesthood, by the total separation of the church from the State …"[16]

There are numerous other writings from Madison where he firmly supported the separation of Church and State. And, as I will show later, Madison's actions as President also proves that he believed strongly in the separation of Church and State. Perhaps the most powerful document *ever* that was written in support of separation of church and state, was written by Madison. In 1785 Madison wrote his famous *Memorial and Remonstrance Against Religious Assessments*, the purpose of which was to oppose a Virginia bill put forward by Patrick Henry and other religious zealots that would have authorized tax support for Christian ministers in the state of Virginia. This piece of writing by Madison is fifteen-point well-crafted rebuttal against any form of alliance between government and religion. A full and complete copy of this document can be found at the end of this Chapter in Appendix 6A. O'Reilly and Religious Conservatives should really read it very carefully before they go around misrepresenting Madison's views on Church and State. In the preamble Madison wrote:

> "We, the subscribers, citizens of the said Commonwealth, having taken in serious consideration, a Bill printed by the order of the last Session of General Assembly, entitled 'A Bill establishing a provision for Teachers of the Christian Religion,' and conceiving that the same, if finally armed with the sanctions of a law, will be a dangerous abuse of power, are bound as faithful members of a free State, to remonstrate against it, and to declare the reasons by which we are determined. We remonstrate against the said Bill,"[17]

The most powerful passage opposing alliance between Church and State is found in section eight, where Madison argued very eloquently that religion is not necessary for Civil Government, and Civil Government must not be intertwined with "ecclesiastical" establishments:

"8. Because the establishment in question is not necessary for the support of Civil Government. If it be urged as necessary for the support of Civil Government only as it is a means of supporting religion, and it be not necessary for the latter purpose, it cannot be necessary for the former. If religion be not within the cognizance of Civil Government, how can its legal establishment be said to be necessary to Civil Government? What influence in fact have ecclesiastical establishments had on Civil Society? In some instances they have been seen to erect a spiritual tyranny on the ruins of Civil authority; in many instances they have been seen upholding the thrones of political tyranny; in no instance they have been seen the guardians of the liberties of the people. Rulers who wished to subvert the public liberty may have found an established clergy convenient auxiliaries. A just government, instituted to secure and perpetuate it, needs them not. Such a government will be best supported by protecting every citizen in the enjoyment of his religion with the same equal hand which protects his person and his property; by neither invading the equal rights of any Sect nor suffering any Sect to invade those of another."[18]

This is pretty powerful stuff coming from Madison. (Again, this is only one paragraph, I urge you to read the entire document in Appendix 6A). It is important to note that even though the issue before him was tax support for *Christian* ministers, Madison took the opportunity to express his opposition to *religion as a whole* encroaching upon Civil Government. He consistently used the broad term of "religion" as opposed to "Christianity", indicating that he was not only against government support for a particular religion—Christianity—but was also against government support of *any* religion. He argued not only that religion is unnecessary for the functioning of Civil Government, but also that "ecclesiastical" establishment's influence on Civil Government leads to political tyranny.

O'Reilly argued that "it is apparent that the Founders wanted very much to keep God in the public arena, even uppermost in the thoughts to the populace."[19], but given Madison's opinion above, how exactly does O'Reilly suggest that America "keep God in the public arena, even uppermost in the thoughts of the populace"? Whose responsibility is it specifically to "keep God in the public arena"? The President? The Congress? The Courts? Someone else? Who? And which religion should we use to "keep God in the public arena"? O'Reilly also did not say what social mechanism(s) the Founding Fathers proposed utilizing to keep God in the public arena. Putting up the Ten Commandments in public places? Have the Bible read in schools? What? How exactly does the government keep God in people's mind? He couldn't cite any means put forth by the Founding Fathers to "keep God in the public arena", because the Founding Fathers never proposed any. The Founding Fathers never prescribed a way to keep God in people's mind, because by definition if the government is not supposed to support any one religion, which O'Reilly sometimes seems to agree with, then it cannot utilize any of those religions to "keep God in the public arena". Hence, it is not the responsibility of the government to keep God in the public arena. By the way, are we allowed to put non-Christian symbols up in public places? If there is a Muslim judge can he or she put up quotes from the Koran in his court the same way Conservatives support putting up the Ten Commandments? Are we allowed to read the Bhagvad Gita in schools the same way Conservatives want the Bible read in schools?

When Madison became president he continued Jefferson's tradition of *not* issuing proclamations for days of fasting and thanksgiving, except for a few occasions when he came under intense pressure from religious groups. Hence, it is clear that he also saw his duties as "temporal" just like Jefferson did. More importantly, however, Madison issued two landmark vetoes on two bills that related to church and state issues, which coincidentally is of particular relevance today. First, On February 21, 1811, he vetoed a bill that would have incorporated an Episcopal Church in the town of Alexander, in the District of Columbia. The proponents of the bill wanted the government to aid a particular church because the church was thought to be doing noble things. He returned the bill to the House of Representatives with the following objections:

> "Having examined and considered the bill entitled 'An Act incorporating the Protestant Episcopal Church in the town of Alexander, in the District of Columbia,' I now return the bill to the House of Representative, in which it originated, with the following objections:
> Because the bill exceeds the rightful authority to which government are limited by the essential distinction between civil and religious functions, and violates in particular the article of the Constitution of the United States which declares 'Congress shall make no law respecting a religious establishment.'....
> ...
> Because the bill vests in the said incorporated church an authority to provide for the support of the poor and the education of poor children of the same, an authority which, being altogether superfluous if the provision is to be the result of pious charity, would be a precedent for giving to religious societies as such a legal agency in carrying into effect a public and civil duty."[20]

Madison's second veto was regarding a bill that would have apportioned government land to a Baptist church in Mississippi. He vetoed the bill on February 28, 1811, and explained his basis for vetoing the bill as follows:

> "Having examined and considered the bill entitled 'An Act for the relief of Richard Trevin, William Coleman, Edward Lewis, Samuel Mims, Joseph Wilson, and the Baptist Church at Salem Meeting House, in the Mississippi Territory.' I now return the same to the House of Representatives, in which it originated, with the following objection:
> Because the bill in reserving a certain parcel of land of the United States for the use of the said Baptist Church comprises a principle and precedent for the appropriation of funds of the United States for the use and support of religious societies, contrary to the article of the Constitution which declares that the 'Congress shall make no law respecting a religious establishment.'"[21]

Based on these two vetoes, there shouldn't be any doubt whatsoever that Madison believed that no form of government assistance should be given to any kind of religious organization, regardless of whether or not the activities of such organization are held to be in the public interest. Hence, even if there is a consensus that certain "faith-based" institutions would better serve the poor than government agencies could, the Constitution of the United States forbids the Congress from making any laws permitting public funds to be allocated to such institutions. O'Reilly and right-wing Conservatives are probably cringing at this, but this is based on *Madison's* interpretation of the Constitution as outlined above, not on the ruling of some "far-left" judge out in San Fransisco.

The other problem with government aiding religious organization, which I would point to, is the potential for corrupting the voters. If politicians go around promising money to religious leaders for their respective organizations, there is the distinct possibility that these religious leaders will begin to take sides in elections and endorse particular candidates in order to get funds from the government for their organization. There is thus the danger that politicians will use the public purse to win votes, leading to political chaos and corruption on a massive scale. This cannot be allowed to happen, because it will subvert the entire electoral process from local to national. A further problem is what process will be used to decide which particular religious organizations get government funds. What criteria should be used to pick one organization over another? I assume the proponents believe that the Congress and the President should be the final arbiter, which means that the decision becomes a political one, and it will sway depending on the political mood of the times. It is quite possible that with say a

Democratic President and a Democratic controlled Congress, they will favor and support religious organizations that are sympathetic to abortion rights and gay rights, for example, and will penalize organizations that are hostile to these rights. At a different time, a Republican President and a Republican controlled Congress may do the reverse. This is definitely a recipe for chaos, so O'Reilly and the Republicans better be careful what they wish for.

Benjamin Franklin

O'Reilly did not hesitate to point out that at the Constitutional Convention in 1787 Benjamin Franklin tabled a motion saying "I therefore beg leave to move—that henceforth, prayers imploring the assistance of Heaven and its blessings on our deliberations, be held in this Assembly every morning before we proceed to business, and that one or more of the clergy of this city be requested to officiate in that service."[22]. But what he did not tell you was that the motion had virtually no support from the other thirty-eight delegates present, except for perhaps two or three delegates who expressed an interest. The motion was never taken up or debated seriously, and hence it was never was adopted. No prayers were held and no clergy was brought in. The issues were vigorously debated, opinions passionately expressed, and resolutions adopted, all without the religious input Conservatives would have liked. It is pretty disingenuous to quote one member of the thirty-nine-member Delegation and proclaim that it represented the view of the entire delegation. This is not to say that Franklin was just an ordinary member whose opinion didn't matter. Franklin was a great man who deserves the utmost respect for his wisdom and accomplishments, and I wouldn't dare to marginalize him. But you cannot say that because he made the speech he did, it represents clear and convincing evidence that the Founding Fathers favored prayers and clergy in public debate, and wanted government involvement in religious issues. Clearly, Franklin was in the minority on this issue; Thomas Jefferson and James Madison did not support the motion.

But I'm glad O'Reilly brought up Franklin's request for prayers and clergy, because apart from the fact that the motion was never adopted and there were no prayers or clergy at the 1787 Convention, it reminds us of the fact that the U.S. Constitution, probably the greatest and most important document in all of history, was debated and drafted without any religious input, at least *public* religious input. I find it hard to understand that if in fact the Founding Fathers were such avid supporters of the idea of "keeping God in the public arena even uppermost in the thoughts of the populace", as O'Reilly and religious Conservatives claim, why did they choose *not* to have clergy and prayer at the Constitutional Convention? Or why did they not insert a clause into the Constitution supporting government involvement in promoting belief in God?

Notwithstanding, elsewhere in Franklin's writings he was less hospitable to religion than O'Reilly portrays him to be. O'Reilly did not give you the full picture; he cherry picked one quote from Franklin that supported his (O'Reilly's) ideological position and paraded it as a synopsis of Franklin's beliefs. Franklin was a much more complex man than O'Reilly's portrait of him. If you read Franklin's Autobiography you will get a more balanced view of who the man was and what he thought of religion. He wasn't the religious zealot O'Reilly is making him out to be. Franklin didn't go to Church! In his Autobiography, Franklin sheds some light on his religious beliefs, and you might be surprised about what he had to say:

"I had been religiously educated as a Presbyterian; and though some of the dogmas of that persuasion, such as the eternal decrees of God, election, reprobation, etc., appeared to me unintelligible, others doubtful, and I early absented myself from the public assemblies of the sect, Sunday being my studying day, I never was without some religious principles. I never doubted, for instance, the existence of the Deity; that he made the world, and governed it by his Providence; that the most acceptable service of God was doing good to man; that our souls are immortal; and that all crime will be punished, and virtue rewarded, either here or hereafter. These I esteemed the essentials of every religion; and, being to be found in all the religions we had in our country, I respected them all, though with different degrees of respect, as I found them more or less mixed with other articles, which, without any tendency to inspire, promote, or confirm morality, served principally to divide us, and make us unfriendly to one another. This respect to all, with an opinion that the worst had some good effects, induced me to avoid all discourse that might tend to lessen the good opinion another might have of his own religion; and as our province increased in people, and new places of worship were continually wanted, and generally erected by voluntary contribution, my mite for such purpose, whatever might be the sect, was never refused.

Though I seldom attended any public worship, I had still an opinion of it's propriety, and it's utility when rightly conducted, and I regularly paid my annual subscription for the support of the only Presbyterian minister or meeting we had in Philadelphia. He used to visit me sometimes as a friend, and admonish me to attend his administrations, and I was now and then prevailed on to do so, once for five Sundays successively. Had he been in my opinion a good preacher, perhaps I might have continued, notwithstanding the occasion I had for the Sunday's leisure in my course of study; but his discourses were chiefly either polemic arguments, or explications of the peculiar doctrines of our sect, and were all to me very dry, uninteresting, and unedifying, since not a single moral principle was inculcated or enforced, their aim seeming to be rather to make us Presbyterian than good citizens.

At length he took for his text that verse of the fourth chapter of Philippians, "Finally, brethren, whatsoever things are true, honest, just, pure, lovely, or of good report, if there be any virtue, or any praise, think on these things." And I imagined, in a sermon on such a text, we could not miss of having some morality. But he confined himself to five points only, as meant by the apostle, viz.: 1. Keeping holy the Sabbath day. 2. Being diligent in reading the holy Scriptures. 3. Attending duly the public worship. 4. Partaking of the Sacrament. 5. Paying a due respect to God's ministries. These might be all good things; but, as they were not the kind of good things I expected from that text, I despaired of ever meeting with them from any other, was disgusted, and attended his preaching no more. I had some years before composed a little Liturgy, or form of prayer, for my own private use (viz., in 1728), entitled, *Articles of Belief and Acts of Religion.* I returned to the use of this, and went no more to the public assemblies. My conduct might be blameable, but I leave it, without attempting further to excuse it; my present purpose being to relate facts, and not to make apologies for them."[23]

Franklin said that he "early absented himself from the public assemblies of the sect". So unlike O'Reilly, Mr. Bush, and other Conservatives, who suit themselves up in the finest on Sundays, clutch their Bibles, and head for the church, Franklin didn't go to church! Franklin found the preachers unimpressive; he felt that they focused on the nuances of their sect rather than on the important moral issues of humankind. Franklin believed that the best service to God was "doing good to man", and he says he always avoided discussion that "lessen the good opinion another might have of his own religion". This is not a man who would have favored religion in the public domain or would have favored the government getting involved in religion. In fact, as I noted in the beginning of this chapter, he believed that if a religion is good it can stand on it's own without government support. O'Reilly has misrepresented the views and beliefs of Benjamin Franklin to support his ideology. When you consider Franklin's views and beliefs on religion in it's totality, you *cannot* conclude that he would have favored government getting involved with religion.

To conclude, based on their writings and their actions, neither Thomas Jefferson, nor James Madison, nor Benjamin Franklin believed that it was the government's role to intervene in religious issues or take the side of any religious organization, or support religion in any way. I have presented the facts of these men's lives as it pertains to their views on Church and State. Overall, they believed that politics didn't need religion and religion didn't need politics, and society would better function if the two are kept separate. O'Reilly and Christian Conservatives are either mistaken or have deliberately distorted the records of these great men to further their own religious agenda. They have focused on the personal beliefs of the Founding Fathers as opposed to the Founding Father's public policy position as incorporated in the Constitution of the United States and demonstrated by the tenures of Jefferson and Madison as third and fourth President respectively. There is no doubt that these two men were skeptical of close ties between Church and State, and believed that Church and State should stay apart from each other for their own good.

Perhaps the most remarkable piece of history associated with Jefferson and Madison in the context of Church and State separation is the founding of the University of Virginia. Thomas Jefferson founded the University of Virginia, in close collaboration with James Madison. One of the founding principles of the University was that it be a secular institution. At that time (early 1800's) other existing American universities were closely tied to religious institutions, since the main purpose of higher education was the instruction of church clergymen. Jefferson, however, believed that the primary focus of education should be scientific knowledge, and in keeping with his view that religious instruction should be kept separate from university studies, he included neither *church* nor *chapel* in his design of the university structure. Instead, he placed the library at the center of the architectural design, physically as well as symbolically. During the entire process Jefferson was in constant contact with Madison, soliciting his advise on everything from the location of the university to the text books that would be made available in the university's library, to the courses that would be taught. In fact, many scholars think that Madison's role in the founding of the University of Virginia has been understated. But what's not in dispute is both men's belief that the university should be kept free from religious influences. For Madison, freedom of religion was involved with freedom of mind, and therefore with what would later be called academic freedom. He stated his views on March 19, 1823 in a letter to Edward Everett, then a professor and later president of Harvard, which was a university under religious control. This letter, I think, proves undisputedly that Madison believed firmly in the strict separation of Church and State, and should end the debate:

> "I am not surprised at the dilemma produced at your University, by making Theological Professorship an integral part of the System. The anticipation of such an one, led to the omission in ours; the Visitors being merely authorized to open a public Hall for religious occasion, under impartial regulations; with the opportunity to different Sects to establish their Theological Schools, so

near that the Students at the University may respectively attend the religious exercises in them. The Village of Charlottesville, where different Religious Worships will be held, is also so near that resort may be conveniently had to them.

A University with Sectarian professorships, becomes of course, a Sectarian Monopoly: with professorships of rival sects, it would be an arena of Theological Gladiators: without any such professorship, it must incur for a time at least, the imputation of irreligious tendencies if not designs. The last difficulty was thought more manageable, than either of the others.

On this view of the subject, there seems to be no alternative but between a public University without Theological professorship, or Sectarian Seminaries without a public University.

I recollect to have seen a great many years ago, a project of a paper by Govr [of New Jersey William] Livingston, father of the present Judge [Henry Brockholst Livingston on the Supreme Court], intended to comprehend and conciliate College Students of every denomination, by a Form composed wholly of texts & phrases of Scripture. If a trial of the expedient was ever made, it must have failed, notwithstanding its winning aspect, from the single cause that many sects reject all set forms of worship.

The difficulty of reconciling the Christian mind to the absence of religious Tuition from a University, established by Law & at the common expense, is probably less with us than with you. **The settled opinion here is that religion is essentially distinct from Civil Govt. and exempt from its cognizance; that a connexion between them is injurious to both; that there are causes in the human breast which ensure the perpetuity of religion without the aid of the law; that rival sects with equal rights, exercise mutual censorships in favor of good morals; that if new sects arise with absurd opinions or overheated imaginations, the proper remedies lie in time, forbearance, and example: that a legal establishment of Religion without toleration, could not be thought of, and with a toleration, is no security for public quiet & harmony, but rather a source itself of discord & animosity; and finally, that these opinions are supported by experience, which has shewn that every relaxation of the Alliance between Law & Religion, from the partial example of Holland, to its consummation in Pennsylvania, N. jersey &c. has been found as safe in practice as it is sound in Theory."[24]**

What a letter. Madison could not have expressed his views on separation of church and state any better. And this is the man that O'Reilly claims favored government involvement in religion? O'Reilly is horribly mistaken. The section in bold at the end was my own emphasis, and I did so because these lines from Madison perfectly encapsulate the reasoning behind the separation of church and state. I hope O'Reilly and Religious Conservatives study it carefully.

APPENDIX 6A

<u>James Madison's Memorial and Remonstrance Against Religious Assessments, 1785.</u>

To the Honorable the General Assembly of the Commonwealth of Virginia A Memorial and Remonstrance

We the subscribers, citizens of the said Commonwealth, having taken into serious consideration, a Bill printed by order of the last Session of General Assembly, entitled "A Bill establishing a provision for Teachers of the Christian Religion," and conceiving that the same if finally armed with the sanctions of a law, will be a dangerous abuse of power, are bound as faithful members of a free State to remonstrate against it, and to declare the reasons by which we are determined. We remonstrate against the said Bill,

1. Because we hold it for a fundamental and undeniable truth, "that religion or the duty which we owe to our Creator and the manner of discharging it, can be directed only by reason and conviction, not by force or violence." The Religion then of every man must be left to the conviction and conscience of every man; and it is the right of every man to exercise it as these may dictate. This right is in its nature an unalienable right. It is unalienable, because the opinions of men, depending only on the evidence contemplated by their own minds cannot follow the dictates of other men: It is unalienable also, because what is here a right towards men, is a duty towards the Creator. It is the duty of every man to render to the Creator such homage and such only as he believes to be acceptable to him. This duty is precedent, both in order of time and in degree of obligation, to the claims of Civil Society. Before any man can be considered as a member of Civil Society, he must be considered as a subject of the Governor of the Universe: And if a member of Civil Society, do it with a saving of his allegiance to the Universal Sovereign. We maintain therefore that in matters of Religion, no man's right is abridged by the institution of Civil Society and that Religion is wholly exempt from its cognizance. True it is, that no other rule exists, by which any question which may divide a Society, can be ultimately determined, but the will of the majority; but it is also true that the majority may trespass on the rights of the minority.

2. Because Religion be exempt from the authority of the Society at large, still less can it be subject to that of the Legislative Body. The latter are but the creatures and vicegerents of the former. Their jurisdiction is both derivative and limited: it is limited with regard to the co-ordinate departments, more necessarily is it limited with regard to the constituents. The preservation of a free Government requires not merely, that the metes and bounds which separate each department of power be invariably maintained; but more especially that neither of them be suffered to overleap the great Barrier which defends the rights of the people. The Rulers who are guilty of such an encroachment, exceed the commission from which they derive their authority, and are Tyrants. The People who submit to it are governed by laws made neither by themselves nor by an authority derived from them, and are slaves.

3. Because it is proper to take alarm at the first experiment on our liberties. We hold this prudent jealousy to be the first duty of Citizens, and one of the noblest characteristics of the late Revolution. The free men of America did not wait till usurped power had strengthened itself by exercise, and entangled the question in precedents. They saw all the consequences in the principle, and they avoided the consequences by denying the principle. We revere this lesson too much soon to forget it. Who does not see that the same authority which can establish Christianity, in exclusion of all other Religions, may establish with the same ease any particular sect of Christians, in exclusion of all other Sects? that the same authority which can force a citizen to contribute three pence only of his property for the support of any one establishment, may force him to conform to any other establishment in all cases whatsoever?

4. Because the Bill violates the equality which ought to be the basis of every law, and which is more indispensable, in proportion as the validity or expediency of any law is more liable to be impeached. If "all men are by nature equally free and independent," all men are to be considered as entering into Society on equal conditions; as relinquishing no more, and therefore retaining no less, one than another, of their natural rights. Above all are they to be considered as retaining an "equal title to the free exercise of Religion according to the dictates of Conscience." Whilst we assert for ourselves a freedom to embrace, to profess and to observe the Religion which we believe to be of divine origin, we cannot deny an equal freedom to those whose minds have not yet yielded to the evi-

dence which has convinced us. If this freedom be abused, it is an offence against God, not against man: To God, therefore, not to man, must an account of it be rendered. As the Bill violates equality by subjecting some to peculiar burdens, so it violates the same principle, by granting to others peculiar exemptions. Are the Quakers and Menonists the only sects who think a compulsive support of their Religions unnecessary and unwarrantable? can their piety alone be entrusted with the care of public worship? Ought their Religions to be endowed above all others with extraordinary privileges by which proselytes may be enticed from all others? We think too favorably of the justice and good sense of these denominations to believe that they either covet pre-eminences over their fellow citizens or that they will be seduced by them from the common opposition to the measure.

5.   Because the Bill implies either that the Civil Magistrate is a competent Judge of Religious Truth; or that he may employ Religion as an engine of Civil policy. The first is an arrogant pretension falsified by the contradictory opinions of Rulers in all ages, and throughout the world: the second an unhallowed perversion of the means of salvation.

6.   Because the establishment proposed by the Bill is not requisite for the support of the Christian Religion. To say that it is, is a contradiction to the Christian Religion itself, for every page of it disavows a dependence on the powers of this world: it is a contradiction to fact; for it is known that this Religion both existed and flourished, not only without the support of human laws, but in spite of every opposition from them, and not only during the period of miraculous aid, but long after it had been left to its own evidence and the ordinary care of Providence. Nay, it is a contradiction in terms; for a Religion not invented by human policy, must have pre-existed and been supported, before it was established by human policy. It is moreover to weaken in those who profess this Religion a pious confidence in its innate excellence and the patronage of its Author; and to foster in those who still reject it, a suspicion that its friends are too conscious of its fallacies to trust it to its own merits.

7.   Because experience witnesseth that ecclesiastical establishments, instead of maintaining the purity and efficacy of Religion, have had a contrary operation. During almost fifteen centuries has the legal establishment of Christianity been on trial. What have been its fruits? More or less in all places, pride and indolence in the Clergy, ignorance and servility in the

laity, in both, superstition, bigotry and persecution. Enquire of the Teachers of Christianity for the ages in which it appeared in its greatest lustre; those of every sect, point to the ages prior to its incorporation with Civil policy. Propose a restoration of this primitive State in which its Teachers depended on the voluntary rewards of their flocks, many of them predict its downfall. On which Side ought their testimony to have greatest weight, when for or when against their interest?

8. Because the establishment in question is not necessary for the support of Civil Government. If it be urged as necessary for the support of Civil Government only as it is a means of supporting Religion, and it be not necessary for the latter purpose, it cannot be necessary for the former. If Religion be not within the cognizance of Civil Government how can its legal establishment be necessary to Civil Government? What influence in fact have ecclesiastical establishments had on Civil Society? In some instances they have been seen to erect a spiritual tyranny on the ruins of the Civil authority; in many instances they have been seen upholding the thrones of political tyranny: in no instance have they been seen the guardians of the liberties of the people. Rulers who wished to subvert the public liberty, may have found an established Clergy convenient auxiliaries. A just Government instituted to secure & perpetuate it needs them not. Such a Government will be best supported by protecting every Citizen in the enjoyment of his Religion with the same equal hand which protects his person and his property; by neither invading the equal rights of any Sect, nor suffering any Sect to invade those of another.

9. Because the proposed establishment is a departure from the generous policy, which, offering an Asylum to the persecuted and oppressed of every Nation and Religion, promised a lustre to our country, and an accession to the number of its citizens. What a melancholy mark is the Bill of sudden degeneracy? Instead of holding forth an Asylum to the persecuted, it is itself a signal of persecution. It degrades from the equal rank of Citizens all those whose opinions in Religion do not bend to those of the Legislative authority. Distant as it may be in its present form from the Inquisition, it differs from it only in degree. The one is the first step, the other the last in the career of intolerance. The magnanimous sufferer under this cruel scourge in foreign Regions, must view the Bill as a Beacon on our Coast, warning him to seek some other

haven, where liberty and philanthropy in their due extent, may offer a more certain repose from his Troubles.

10. Because it will have a like tendency to banish our Citizens. The allurements presented by other situations are every day thinning their number. To superadd a fresh motive to emigration by revoking the liberty which they now enjoy, would be the same species of folly which has dishonoured and depopulated flourishing kingdoms

11. Because it will destroy that moderation and harmony which the forbearance of our laws to intermeddle with Religion has produced among its several sects. Torrents of blood have been split in the old world, by vain attempts of the secular arm, to extinguish Religious discord, by proscribing all difference in Religious opinion. Time has at length revealed the true remedy. Every relaxation of narrow and rigorous policy, wherever it has been tried, has been found to assuage the disease. The American Theatre has exhibited proofs that equal and compleat liberty, if it does not wholly eradicate it, sufficiently destroys its malignant influence on the health and prosperity of the State. If with the salutary effects of this system under our own eyes, we begin to contract the bounds of Religious freedom, we know no name that will too severely reproach our folly. At least let warning be taken at the first fruits of the threatened innovation. The very appearance of the Bill has transformed "that Christian forbearance, love and charity," which of late mutually prevailed, into animosities and jealousies, which may not soon be appeased. What mischiefs may not be dreaded, should this enemy to the public quiet be armed with the force of a law?

12. Because the policy of the Bill is adverse to the diffusion of the light of Christianity. The first wish of those who enjoy this precious gift ought to be that it may be imparted to the whole race of mankind. Compare the number of those who have as yet received it with the number still remaining under the dominion of false Religions; and how small is the former! Does the policy of the Bill tend to lessen the disproportion? No; it at once discourages those who are strangers to the light of revelation from coming into the Region of it; and countenances by example the nations who continue in darkness, in shutting out those who might convey it to them. Instead of Levelling as far as possible, every obstacle to the victorious progress of Truth, the Bill with an ignoble and unchris-

tian timidity would circumscribe it with a wall of defence against the encroachments of error.

13. Because attempts to enforce by legal sanctions, acts obnoxious to go great a proportion of Citizens, tend to enervate the laws in general, and to slacken the bands of Society. If it be difficult to execute any law which is not generally deemed necessary or salutary, what must be the case, where it is deemed invalid and dangerous? And what may be the effect of so striking an example of impotency in the Government, on its general authority?

14. Because a measure of such singular magnitude and delicacy ought not to be imposed, without the clearest evidence that it is called for by a majority of citizens, and no satisfactory method is yet proposed by which the voice of the majority in this case may be determined, or its influence secured. The people of the respective counties are indeed requested to signify their opinion respecting the adoption of the Bill to the next Session of Assembly." But the representatives or of the Counties will be that of the people. Our hope is that neither of the former will, after due consideration, espouse the dangerous principle of the Bill. Should the event disappoint us, it will still leave us in full confidence, that a fair appeal to the latter will reverse the sentence against our liberties.

15. Because finally, "the equal right of every citizen to the free exercise of his Religion according to the dictates of conscience" is held by the same tenure with all our other rights. If we recur to its origin, it is equally the gift of nature; if we weigh its importance, it cannot be less dear to us; if we consult the "Declaration of those rights which pertain to the good people of Virginia, as the basis and foundation of Government," it is enumerated with equal solemnity, or rather studied emphasis. Either the, we must say, that the Will of the Legislature is the only measure of their authority; and that in the plenitude of this authority, they may sweep away all our fundamental rights; or, that they are bound to leave this particular right untouched and sacred: Either we must say, that they may control the freedom of the press, may abolish the Trial by Jury, may swallow up the Executive and Judiciary Powers of the State; nay that they may despoil us of our very right of suffrage, and erect themselves into an independent and hereditary Assembly or, we must say, that they have no authority to enact into the law the Bill under consideration.

We the Subscribers say, that the General Assembly of this Commonwealth have no such authority: And that no effort may be omitted on our part against so dangerous an usurpation, we oppose to it, this remonstrance; earnestly praying, as we are in duty bound, that the Supreme Lawgiver of the Universe, by illuminating those to whom it is addressed, may on the one hand, turn their Councils from every act which would affront his holy prerogative, or violate the trust committed to them: and on the other, guide them into every measure which may be worthy of his [blessing, may re] dound to their own praise, and may establish more firmly the liberties, the prosperity and the happiness of the Commonwealth.

Footnotes to Chapter Six

1) Who's Looking Out for You, Bill O'Reilly, page 114.

2) Who's Looking Out for You, Bill O'Reilly, page 114.

3) Who's Looking Out for You, Bill O'Reilly, page 117.

4) Who's Looking Out for You, Bill O'Reilly, page 116.

5) Thomas Jefferson's letter to Baron von Humboldt, 1813.

6) The Founding Fathers, A Biography in His Own Words, James Madison, page 381-82.

7) Benjamin Franklin's letter to Richard Price, October 9, 1780.

8) Who's Looking Out for You, Bill O'Reilly, page 116.

9) The Republic of Letters, The Correspondences between Jefferson and Madison 1776-1826, Volume One, page 394.

10) Who's Looking Out for You, Bill O'Reilly, page 113.

11) Elementary School Act, Thomas Jefferson, 1817.

12) Note to Elementary School Act, Thomas Jefferson, 1817.

13) Who's Looking Out for You, Bill O'Reilly, page 117.

14) Who's Looking Out for You, Bill O'Reilly, page 117.

15) Who's Looking Out for You, Bill O'Reilly, page 117.

16) James Madison's Letter to Robert Walsh, March 2, 1819

17) The Complete Madison, His Basic Writings, Saul K. Padover, page 299.

18) Memorial and Remonstrance against Religious Assessments, James Madison, 1785.

19) Who's Looking Out for You, Bill O'Reilly, page 114.

20) James Madison, 1751—1836, Edited by Ian Elliot, page 59.

21) The Complete Madison, His Basic Writings, Saul K. Padover, page 308.

22) Who's Looking Out for You, Bill O'Reilly, page 116.

23) Benjamin Franklin's Autobiography, page 91-92.

24) The Founding Fathers, A Biography in His Own Words, James Madison, page 381-82.

7

Bill Clinton And September 11ᵗʰ

"The result was that Mr. Clinton and his security advisers were shut out of information about terrorism domestically by Freeh and internationally by the insane Torricelli Principle. And many of us wonder how September 11 could have happened?"[1]

Fact: The 9/11 Commission found no evidence to support the claim that any action taken by Mr. Clinton during his tenure weakened the intelligence services in any way or prevented them from performing their duty.

Did you notice how Bill O'Reilly links President Clinton to September 11ᵗʰ in the above quote? Very sneaky, isn't it? But we cannot let him get away with it so easily. This goes back to what I said in Chapter One about the techniques he uses. Here he uses the two techniques of *Association* and *Fabrication* to connect Mr. Clinton to the 9/11 tragedy. Although the tragedy occurred *nine months* into the presidency of George W. Bush, O'Reilly specifically blames Bill Clinton, *and only Bill Clinton*, for the attack. O'Reilly ignores all of the facts and cooks up two bizarre theories to implicate Mr. Clinton in the failings of *both* the CIA and the FBI. Very convenient, isn't it?

The CIA

Regarding the CIA, O'Reilly argued that the CIA failed to infiltrate Al Qaeda and obtain advance information on the 9/11 attacks because Mr. Clinton tied the hands of the CIA when he consented to the "Torricelli Principle" back in 1996. What is the "Torricelli Principle"? Well, I let Bill O'Reilly explain:

"Here's how bad it really is. Corruption, incompetence and political correctness have spread like the Ebola virus throughout our federal system, and lack of a disciplined approach to controlling our enemies and securing our borders is one of the main reasons that three thousand Americans were murdered on September 11, 2001. To understand what happened we have to go back to 1996 and peek into an Oval Office meeting between the aforementioned President Clinton and Senator Torricelli.

Called "The Torch" because of his volcanic temper, New Jersey's former senator deftly cultivated a neoliberal political persona that mixed pragmatism with pandering. Because New Jersey is home to hundreds of thousands of newly arrived Hispanic immigrants, Torricelli played to the home team and became deeply involved with a variety of issues that struck emotional chords with the new citizens.

In 1995, a Guatemalan colonel named Julio Roberto Alpirez was linked to the murder of an American in that chaotic country. For decades the Guatemalan army had been systemically assassinating leftist rebel leaders and those who they thought supported them. Alpirez apparently controlled some of these death squads even as he was on the CIA payroll as an informer, a situation not uncommon the world over. Throughout the Cold War, the Central Intelligence Agency often paid rightist thugs for information that could be used against Communist agitators. The CIA calls these informants "assets".

Anyway, Torricelli, then a congressman, went public with the story, embarrassed the CIA, and enlisted President Clinton to "reform" the informer payroll. Sensing political gain, Mr. Clinton ordered the CIA to stop paying any informer suspected of human rights violations or who had a felony conviction on his record. Any exceptions had to be approved by the CIA brass in Langley, Virginia. President Clinton's order became knows as "the Torricelli Principle."

Within months, U.S. ground intelligence virtually dried up. Scores of CIA station chiefs submitted their retirement papers, knowing that they could not gather intelligence as effectively as they had during the Cold War. Without the criminal element informing on the criminal element, the CIA became deaf. Bad people know what other bad people are doing. Mother Teresa does not.

These grizzled veterans who retired from the Agency were often replaced by young officers with little or no field experience and no contacts in the shadowy world of counterintelligence. Thus Osama Bin Laden and his murderous zealots developed Al Qaeda with little scrutiny from the CIA. By presidential mandate the U.S. national security apparatus could not associate with terrorists who might have infiltrated the group or even pay for information about it. Al Qaeda managed to bomb two U.S. embassies and the USS Cole with few problems because our federal government had minimal intelligence on the missions.

Incredibly, even after those attacks, the Torricelli Principle remained in place. It was only after the catastrophe on September 11 that President Bush ordered it out of existence."[2]

The key sentence in the above quote is "To understand what happened we have to go back to 1996 and peek into an Oval Office meeting between the afore-mentioned President Clinton and Senator Torricelli." So right there O'Reilly starts to lay the foundation for blaming Mr. Clinton for the intelligence failures pre 9/11. But the fundamental problem with O'Reilly's thesis is this: He is claim-ing that Mr. Clinton destroyed something that never really existed. He wants you to believe that prior to 1996 U.S. intelligence services were making tremendous progress penetrating Al Qaeda and other terrorist groups, and then suddenly in 1996 Mr. Clinton pulled the rug out from under and stopped everything dead in their tracks. But the fact of the matter is that U.S. intelligence services were *never* able to infiltrate Islamic terrorist groups. That was true prior to 1996, it was true after 1996, and it is still true today even after September 11, 2001 with the Patriot Act in place and an all out war on terror. To make my case regarding pre-1996 intelligence failures, I would firstly point to the first World Trade Center bombing, which O'Reilly conveniently neglected to mention in his theory above, because obviously it doesn't support his hypothesis. That attack occurred on Feb-ruary 26, 1993, and here is how former counter-terrorism expert Richard Clark, who served seven presidents and worked inside the White House for George H.W. Bush, Bill Clinton, and George W. Bush, described the chaos of February 26, 1993 in his book *Against All Enemies*:

> "The large, white telephone console blurted. I had never heard it ring before and wasn't initially sure what the noise was. In the little window on the con-sole a name popped up: 'Snowcroft.' Brent Snowcroft, the National Security Advisor to the first President Bush, had left the White House the month before, along with almost all of his staff except me and a few other holdovers. How was he calling me now on this highly secure phone? I reached for the handset.
> 'Did the Serbs bomb it?' It was Tony. I had no idea what he was talking about. 'Did the Serbs bomb it? Was it a bomb?'
> 'I don't know yet, Tony,' I faked it. 'We're checking. Let me get back to you as soon as we have something, soon.'
> My next call was to the Situation Room. 'Did something just get bombed?'
> 'Well, something just exploded, we don't know if it was a bomb, Sir. The World Trade Center,' a young Navy officer replied.[3]

The "Tony" Richard Clarke refers to above is Tony Lake, the then National Security Adviser to President Clinton. Tony Lake didn't have the slightest idea who carried out the bombing, and so did everyone else in the administration. No one has disputed Mr. Clarke's account of the events on that fateful day, and it is common knowledge that U.S. intelligence services were clueless when the attack initially occurred. It was only by a stroke of luck that the FBI was able to crack the case open. Had Mohammed Salameh not decided on March 4, 1993 to go back to DIB Leasing in Jersey City, New Jersey, to claim his $400.00 deposit on the Ford Econoline cargo van he had rented, and decided instead to fly out to Germany on March 5 as he had planned, we may never have know the facts of the attack until this day. (You may remember that agents were waiting for Salameh at DIB Leasing, and that is how he was caught). How then can O'Reilly claim that prior to 1996 U.S. intelligence services were better placed to infiltrate terrorist groups than after 1996? The events of February 26, 1993 clearly disprove O'Reilly's theory. Hence, his claim that prior to 1996 U.S. intelligence services were making progress in the infiltration of Islamic terrorist groups, and Mr. Clinton's implementation of the "Torrecelli Principle" in 1996 subsequently obliterated the progress made, is without merit. What is he talking about when he says "Within months, U.S ground intelligence virtually dried up"? What intelligence, Mr. O'Reilley? How come the terrorists were able to plan and carry out the first World Trade Center bombing without anyone in the U.S. intelligence services knowing anything about it, Sir? There was no "Torrecelli Principle" in effect back then. If O'Reilly's assertions were true, shouldn't the CIA have had at least some hunch that something was up? The CIA didn't, so right there, O'Reilly's theory collapses on its face.

O'Reilly chose to zero in on the "Torrecelli Principle" and argues that *it* was the fundamental problem with the U.S. intelligence system, but yet no senior CIA official agrees with him on that count. Senior CIA officials have never complained that they were constrained by the new directive. In his testimony before the 9/11 Commission, George Tenet did not complain about the Torrecilli Principle, but instead talked about the progress the CIA had made. He did not complain at all about being restricted by U.S. law in building intelligence capabilities:

> "To penetrate Bin Ladin's sanctuary, we also worked with Central Asian intelligence services and with the Northern Alliance and its leader, Ahmed Shah Massoud, on everything from technical collection to building an intelligence capability to potential renditions. And we developed a network of agents inside Afghanistan who were directed to track Bin Ladin. We worked with friendly tribal partners for years to undertake operations against him.
> Our human intelligence rose markedly from 1999 through 2001. By September 11ᵗʰ, a map of Afghanistan would show that these collection programs, human networks, were in place in numbers to nearly cover the country. The array meant that when the military campaign to topple and destroy the Taliban began in October of 2001, we were able to support it with an enormous

body of information and a large stable of assets. These networks gave us the platform from which to launch the rapid take-down of the Taliban ..."[4]

O'Reilly also doesn't seem to understand the difficulties involved in infiltrating an organization like Al Qaeda. You infiltrate an organization in basically two ways. First, you can try to have your guy or gal pose as a sympathetic figure and befriend members of the organization and ultimately sign up as a member. Then, being a member, and having access to useful information, he or she then finds a way to pass that information back to you. This is an extremely difficult task, because not only do you have to convince the leadership of the organization that you believe in it's mission (even thought you deeply in your heart loath the organization), but you also have to be willing to submit yourself to whatever test they decide to put you through, thereby betraying your own conscience and possibly doing things you strongly believe in your heart to be immoral and inhumane, not to mention risking your life.

In the context of the United States and Al Qaeda, infiltrating Al Qaeda means that the United States have to find suitable *loyal* individuals who are willing to risk their lives joining the ranks of Al Qaeda and passing information back to the CIA. Such individuals at a minimum have to speak and understand Arabic in order to be able to successfully understand the discussions going on in the network, and also to be able talk to other members to glean sensitive information. How many Americans do we have that are willing and capable to accept such a mission? Using a traditional double agent like the old Cold War days is unlikely to be successful, since Al Qaeda is very different from the former Soviet Union in many ways. Race and Culture are two primary factors that make it very difficult for traditional old style infiltration of Al Qaeda by U.S. intelligence services. Successful infiltration of Al Qaeda ideally requires an Arab-American male who is solidly loyal to America, who is in his heart opposed to the ideology of Bin Ladin, and above all one who is willing to risk his life and make the necessary sacrifices for the sake of America. It is extremely difficult if not impossible to find such a creature in the United States. If O'Reilly knows of any such individual I bet the CIA will pay him big bucks to recruit him.

The other thing you can do is try to get a Muslim in a foreign country to do the job—offer him a few hundred grand and hope for the best. But the fundamental problem is that Muslims are very loyal individuals. They would very rarely turn against a fellow Muslim simply for money. We see evidence of that today with the bounty of twenty five million dollars on Usama Bin Ladin, but yet no solid leads to find him, despite the fact that there are people who know where he is but for twenty five million dollars they are not prepared to sell him out.

The CIA, though, did have some Muslim human intelligence people on the ground in Afghanistan from the Northern Alliance providing them with information on Al Qaeda and Bin Ladin. As a matter of fact, the CIA did gain substantial information that resulted in some limited actions against Bin Ladin, which we will get into in Chapter Eight, but unfortunately that information did not take them into the 9/11 plot itself.

The second way to infiltrate an organization is to get in touch with existing members and simply bribe them (with money) to sell out and provide you the information you need. But with Al Qaeda this is just not a possibility. As I described above, twenty five million dollars are being offered for Bin Ladin but the Muslims who know where he is remain absolutely loyal to him and are not swayed by twenty five million dollars. In this case money simply cannot get you what you need.

Given these difficulties infiltrating Al Qaeda, it is clear that Torrecelli Principle or not, it is very difficult for U.S. intelligence services to gain advance knowledge of terrorist plots. The implementation of the Torrecelli Principle in 1996 was simply not an equation of any significance, as O'Reilly wants you to believe. He is simply looking for something to blame Mr. Clinton for. His hatred for Mr. Clinton is so deep that he would grab at anything to blame Mr. Clinton and tarnish his reputation. This has been O'Reilly's strategy in almost every presentation he has done on President Clinton, so we shouldn't be surprised.

Finally, O'Reilly says above that Mr. Bush ordered the Torrecelli Principle out of existence after September 11, 2001, so my question is: What difference has it made, Mr. O'Reilly? Here we are five plus years into the new era but terrorist incidents are on the rise worldwide. This proves my case that the Torrecelli Principle had no effect one way or the other on intelligence gathering pertaining to Islamic terrorist groups.

The FBI

O'Reilly similarly wasted no time blaming President Clinton also for the alleged failure of the FBI. Here is what he had to say:

> "The FBI endured a similar situation under President Clinton. Because Mr. Clinton and then FBI chief Louis Freeh despised each other, little information was shared between the Bureau and the Executive Branch. Early in the Clinton administration, Director Freeh was deeply embarrassed that FBI files

found their way into the hands of the Clintons at the White House. Some believe those files were copied and later used for political purposes.

Even worse, Freeh knew that Attorney General Janet Reno was blocking all the campaign-finance-related investigations involving the President and Vice President, and all evidence that Mr. Clinton and Al Gore were lying to the American people was being systematically buried by the Justice Department. The bitterness between Freeh and Clinton is documented in the book Age of Sacred Terror, written by two counterterrorism experts who worked for Clinton's national security team. They accurately report that Freeh simply would not tell the White House anything relevant about specific terrorism intelligence that the bureau had developed. The result was that Mr. Clinton and his security advisers were shut out of information about terrorism domestically by Freeh and internationally by the insane Torricelli Principle. And many of us wonder how September 11 could have happened?"[5]

Just like his first thesis regarding the failure of the CIA, O'Reilly's thesis regarding the failure of the FBI is lacking in logic and empirical evidence. He is basically saying that one of the reasons 9/11 occurred was because Mr. Freeh and Mr. Clinton did not talk to each other. Do you really believe that Mr. Freeh had important information about terrorist plots or the like and simply couldn't be bothered to tell anyone in the Clinton Administration, because he despised them so much? That would be highly irresponsible of Mr. Freeh if it were true, don't you think? O'Reilly is basically accusing Mr. Freeh of deliberate dereliction of duty. He says '… Mr. Clinton and his security advisers were shut out of information about terrorism domestically by Freeh …' And he levels the accusation without providing any specifics to back up his claim. What exactly did Mr. Freeh know and didn't pass on to Mr. Clinton? O'Reilly sights the book written by Daniel Benjamin and Steven Simon entitled *The Age Of Sacred Terror* to support his assertion that Freeh refused to communicate with the Clinton Administration because Freeh was embarrassed about the various investigations that were going on against the Clinton Administration. This book is a 445 page account that brilliantly chronicles Islamic Terrorism and provides insightful details on the workings of the American Government vis-à-vis the rise of Islamic terrorism. Here is what the book had to say regarding Mr. Freeh's attitude towards the Clinton White House:

> "In the 1990's, an additional factor contributed to the overall problems of dealing with the Bureau: Louis Freeh's animus towards the White House. Throughout Feeeh's tenure, White House officials found that the FBI director did not feel that the same rules applied to him as to other top government officials: he refused, for example, to come to meetings on the weekend and, to

demonstrate his independence of the nation's political leaders, he turned in his White House pass, saying that he would go there only as a visitor. (The gesture was a strange and hallow one; the Secret Service Uniform Division personnel who guarded the White House identify all senior officials by sight and do not require badges.) The relationship between the director and 1600 Pennsylvania Avenue took on the hue of personal antipathy early on. Most within the White House dated the hostility to Clinton's first term, when the special investigation into Whitewater began expanding to include Filegate, Travelgate, and the billing practices at Hilary Clinton's Little Rock law firm. Freeh himself dated much of the dissatisfaction to the White House handling of the Khobar Towers bombing. He took a passionate interest in the case, and within the Bureau there was admiration for his dedication and some bemusement at the director who had become the case agent-in-chief. The investigation stalled quickly, because the Saudis refused to allow the FBI access to suspects....."[6]

Now, reading the above paragraph, I came away with the understanding that there are two different opinions regarding Mr. Freeh's attitude towards the White House: firstly the White House people believing that it was to do with the investigations into the Clinton Administration, and secondly, Mr. Freeh himself who says it was to do with the White House's handling of the Khobar Towers bombing. This doesn't prove that Mr. Freeh and the Clinton Administration did not communicate on crucial matters that would have probably prevented 9/11, assuming such information did exist. Also, it doesn't specifically say what Mr. Freeh knew and didn't tell Mr. Clinton that would have prevented 9/11. So whatever the reason for the bad relationship between the FBI Director and the White House, assuming there was in fact a bad relationship, that doesn't in itself explain anything about 9/11, unless O'Reilly can provide a specific instance where better communication between the FBI and the Clinton Administration could have prevented 9/11. He did not, and cannot.

One other fact worth noting is that, unlike President George W. Bush who received his briefings via face-to-face meetings with the CIA and the FBI, Mr. Clinton received his daily briefings in writing, and would scribble back notes to either the CIA or the FBI if he needed further information or have questions that he needed answers to. Hence, the fact that Mr. Freeh did not meet *personally* with Mr. Clinton a lot does not mean that information wasn't flowing between the FBI and the White House. Furthermore, let's not forget that the 9/11 tragedy occurred nine months after Mr. Clinton left office. One would assume that if in fact the FBI and the Clinton White House did not communicate, for whatever reason, and once the Administration changed, and the Bush Administration came in, the "communication" problem would have been solved and they would have been working together for the nine months prior to 9/11. This would be a fair assumption to make, would it not? Hence, O'Reilly's claim would have had more validity had the attacks occurred while Mr. Clinton was still in office, because then one can say that there was probably some crucial information that didn't pass from the FBI to the Administration, which led to inaction, and which in turn resulted in the tragedy. But the fact that the tragedy occurred nine months after Mr. Clinton left office, and the FBI had a new administration to work with, totally invalidates O'Reilly claims, because presumably nothing was in the way of communication between the Bush White House and the FBI, right?

The Facts About Intelligence Failures Prior To 9/11

The 9/11 Commission did not find any evidence to support the claim made by Bill O'Reilly and other right-wing nuts that specific policies and actions by President Clinton contributed to the failure of intelligence prior to 9/11. The failure of intelligence was mainly to do with internal failings within the CIA and the FBI and the lack of cooperation and communication between these two agencies. Here are some of the important facts, none of which had anything to do with Bill Clinton:

1) The CIA lost track of Khalid al Mihdar and failed to put him on a watch list

The U.S. State Department maintains a database called the TIPOFF system, which is essentially a list of persons who are of interest to law enforcement authorities in the United States. Visa Officers at U.S. embassies and consulates abroad utilize this database to vet visa applicants to ensure that visas are not issued to individuals on the watch list, and hence prevent dangerous individuals from getting U.S. visas. Similarly, Immigration Officials at U.S. ports of entry also have access to this database, which enables them to vet incoming passengers and deny entry to anyone on the watch list or detain them for questioning.

Khalid al Mihdar was a hijacker aboard American Airlines Flight 77 that crashed into the Pentagon. The CIA actually first learned about Mihdar back in late 1999 when the National Security Agency (NSA) was analyzing communication associated with three Arab men. The communications involved a man by the name of "Khalid", a man by the name of "Nawaf", and a man by the name of "Salem". So at first Mihdar was known only as "Khalid" by the CIA. But in early January 2000 the CIA was able to obtain a photograph of Mihdar's Saudi passport, which provided them with Mihdar's full name and other details, and more importantly they (the CIA) learnt that Mihdar was issued a multiple entry visa by the United States consulate in Jeddah, Saudi Arabia in April 1999.

The CIA had been tracking Mihdar. On Janyary 5, 2000 he was located leaving Yemen and tracked until he arrived in Kuala Lumpur, Malaysia, where he met with a group of other Arab men. Then, suddenly on January 8, 2000 Mihdar and two other Arab men left Kuala Lumpur for Bangkok, Thailand. One of the men was later identified as "Alhazmi", and the other as "Salahase". But in Bangkok, CIA officers received the information too late to track the three men as they came in, so they disappeared into the streets of Bangkok. Incredibly, having lost track of Mihdar and knowing that he possessed a U.S. visa, the CIA did not put Mihdar on the watch list nor did they notify the FBI to look for Mihdar in the U.S.A. Mihdar eventually entered the United States on January 15, 2000 without any trouble, and no one was looking for him.
(Nothing to do with Bill Clinton)

2) Nawaf al Hazmi too slips through the system

Nawaf al Hazmi was also a hijacker aboard American Airlines flight 77 which crashed into the Pentagon. In early March 2000, CIA officers in Bangkok reported back to their colleagues in Kuala Lumpur that "Nawaf Al Hamzi" had departed Bangkok on January 15, 2000 on a United Airlines flight to Los Angeles. Even though the CIA had this information, they did not realize the significance of the name at the time. They did not put two and two together and figured out that the "Nawaf" the NSA was analyzing back in late 1999 and the "Alhazmi" that traveled with Mihdar to Bangkok on January 8, 2000 (mentioned in pt. 1 above) was the same person. Had the CIA sufficiently researched the identities of "Nawaf" and "Alhazmi" they probably would have concluded that it was the same person and his name was Nawaf al Hazmi. Since the CIA did not realize the significance of the name when they received the report from their Bangkok station, they did not put Nawaf al Hazmi on the watch list, and they did not notify the FBI about Al Hazmi's entry into the U.S. Al Hazmi entered the U.S on January 15, 2000 on the same flight with Mihdar.
(Nothing to do with Bill Clinton)

3) The CIA failed to share critical information with the FBI

Based on their interrogation of a captured suspect in the U.S.S. Cole bombing investigation, the CIA learned of the captured suspect's connection to an individual by the name of "Khallad". In December 2000, the CIA's Bin Ladin Unit theorized that Khallad and Khalid al Mihdar (mentioned in 1 above) was probably the same person. In early January 2001, to test their theory, the CIA decided to show two photos from the Kuala Lumpur surveillance to a source who had previously identified Khallad. One photo was a known photo of Khalid Al Mihdar, and the other was an unknown individual who was present at the Kuala Lumpur meeting with Khalid al Mihdar. To the surprise of the CIA, the source did not recognize the photo of Khalid al Mihdar, but identified the previously unknown individual as Khallad. This meant two things: Firstly, Khallad and Khalid al Mihdar were two different people; and secondly, Khalid al Mihdar and Kallad were connected, since they were both present at the Kuala Lumpur meeting on January 5, 2000. This made it all the more important to look for Mihdar, but the CIA still at that point did not put him on the watch list, and did not advise the FBI to look for him in the United States, even though, as we noted above, the CIA knew that Mihdar possessed a U.S. visa.

In the context of the Cole investigation which the FBI was heavily involved with at the time, this was critical new information, but the CIA did not share this new information with the FBI, so the FBI did not start looking for Mihdar. During this entire time Mihdar was in the United States. In June 2000 Mihdar left California and returned to Yemen. On July 4, 2001 Mihdar returned back to the United States. Had the CIA placed him on the State Department TIPOFF watch list he might have been found either when he applied for a new visa in June 2001 or when he physically retuned to the United States on July 4, 2001.
(Nothing to do with Bill Clinton)

4) Lack of cooperation and understanding between the CIA and the FBI

In June 2001, a CIA analyst and an FBI analyst who were both pursuing a suspect in the U.S.S. Cole investigation, decided to show some photos to FBI agents in New York who were also working on the Cole case. The FBI analyst obtained three photos from a CIA official detailed to the International Terrorism Operations Section at the FBI. Again, the photos were from the Kuala Lumpur surveillance that took place in January 2000. While the CIA analyst whom the FBI analyst was teaming up with knew all about the Kuala Lumpur surveillance, the FBI analyst was unaware of its significance. The FBI analyst was told that one of the photos was that of Khalid al Mihdar, but she did not know why the photos were taken or why the Kuala Lumpur meeting might be important. In the end, the New York FBI agents left the meeting without obtaining information that might have started them looking for Mihdar. The CIA analyst who was sitting right there knew Mihdar possessed a U.S. visa, that his visa application indicated he intended to travel to New York, that a source had put Mihdar in the company

of Khallad, and that Nawaf al Hazmi had traveled to Los Angeles, but he did not volunteer any information. He told investigators that as a CIA analyst, he was not authorized to answer FBI questions regarding CIA information. And no one at the meeting asked him to tell what he knew. The FBI analyst said she had assumed that if the CIA analyst knew the answers to questions he would have volunteered them. This was another chance for the FBI and the CIA to pool their intelligence and catch Kalid Al Midhar, but it didn't happen, and Mihdar reentered the United States, flying to New York City on July 4, 2001. No one was looking for him, as I already noted in point three above.
(Nothing to do with Bill Clinton)

5) The Phoenix Memo
    In July 2001 an agent in the FBI field office in Phoenix, Arizona, sent a memo to FBI headquarters and to two international terrorism squads in the New York Field Office advising them of the possibility that Bin Ladin might be sending terrorists to undergo flight training in the USA. The agent based his assessment on FBI findings in Arizona that there were individuals sympathetic to Bin Ladin attending civil aviation schools in Arizona, one such individual being Zacarias Moussaoui (who became knows as the "20th hijacker").
    The agent made four recommendations to FBI headquarters:
—Establish a list of civil aviation schools
—Open up a dialogue with those schools
—Disseminate his theory to the intelligence community
—Seek authority to obtain visa information on individuals applying for training in flight schools.
    However, none of the agent's recommendations were followed. Senior management at FBI headquarters did not even see the memo prior to 9/11, and the New York Field Office took no action. The agent who sent the memo marked it "routine", which meant that it was not top priority.
(Nothing to do with Bill Clinton)

6) George Tenet was briefed on the Moussaoui case but did nothing about it
    On August 23, 2001 George Tenet was briefed about the Moussaoui case in a briefing titled "Islamic Extremist Learns to Fly". He was told that Moussaoui wanted to learn to fly a 747 and paid for his training in cash, and that the FBI had arrested him for visa overstay. Tenet told the 9/11 Commission that at the time there was no established link between Moussaoui and Al Qaeda, so he (Tenet) did not connect the Moussaoui case with the threat reporting during the

summer of 2001. He said that he saw the case as an FBI case and did not discuss the matter further with anyone at the White House or at FBI.
(Nothing to do with Bill Clinton)

It is a fact that both the investigation of the Congress of the United States and the investigation of the 9/11 Commission did not uncover any evidence to prove that Mr. Clinton was at fault for the failures of the CIA or the FBI. O'Reilly's assertions are based on ideology, not on facts. As I will show in the next chapter, Mr. Clinton in fact did pursue policies that strengthened these organizations and boosted their counter terrorism efforts.

Footnotes to Chapter Seven

1) Who's Looking Out for You, Bill O'Reilly, page 40-41.

2) Who's Looking Out for You, Bill O'Reilly, page 38-40.

3) Against All Enemies, Richard Clarke.

4) The 9/11 Commission: Staff Statements and Testimony, page 147.

5) Who's Looking Out for You, Bill O'Reilly, page 40-41.

6) The Age Of Sacred Terror, Daniel Benjamin and Steven Simon.

8

Al Qaeda And The Blame Game

"On his watch, Al Qaeda grew in ferocity and power."[1]

I guess you already know who the "his" refers to in the above quote from Bill O'Reilly, don't you? Yes, you're right, it is Bill Clinton. O'Reilly is always on the lookout to find stuff he can blame Mr. Clinton for. Here he uses the technique of *oversimplification*, and casts blame without providing context. The fact is that pre 9/11, neither the American public (including Bill O'Reilly and many other Conservatives), nor the Congress of the United States, nor the Arab World, nor the international community, would have supported a U.S. invasion of Afghanistan, and for anyone to claim otherwise is totally disingenuous. The question then has to be: Within that context, did the Clinton Administration do all that they could to fight Al Qaeda?

But of course Bill O'Reilly is the typical Monday-Morning Quarterback. What else would you expect? He loves to second-guess the people he disagrees with, and he always creates a big drama after the fact, and pretends that he had known what had to be done. He does this every day on his television program. But we all know that it is just a stunt, and has no meaning in the practical world. O'Reilly talks with great certitude and acts like he knows everything and has the solution to every problem. But prior to 9/11 I've never heard him advocate the invasion of Afghanistan, the overthrow of the Taliban, and the hunting down of Bin Ladin. I have nothing against Monday-Morning Quarterbacks, like Bill O'Reilly, as long as their analysis is fair to the parties involved. But when they engage in dishonest analysis, as in the case of O'Reilly insinuating that Mr. Clinton did *nothing* while Al Qaeda became powerful, the Monday-Morning Quarterback has to be called to account for his bias.

O'Reilly's bias is startling. He refuses to assign any culpability whatsoever to George W. Bush for not stopping Al Qaeda, even though the records show that for nine months Mr. Bush did practically nothing despite warnings from the U.S. intelligence services and his security advisers. Fair and Balanced, do you think? One could equally make a case against Mr. Bush for his failure to deal with Al Qaeda:

—On October 12, 2000 the U.S.S. Cole was bombed in Aden, Yemen, killing 17 sailors and injuring 39 others. Initially US intelligence sources weren't sure who carried out the atrocity, but in the early months of the Bush Administration the intelligence services concluded that Al Qaeda was responsible. Mr. Bush took no retaliatory action against Al Qaeda, even though back in October 2000 when the attack occurred the then Candidate Bush told CNN that "I hope we can gather enough intelligence to figure out who did the act and take the necessary action. There must be a consequence." Mr. Bush obviously did not follow his words with action and Al Qaeda was let off the hook.

—Mr. Bush, then Candidate Bush, began receiving intelligence briefing on terrorism and Al Qaeda as early as September 2000 from the CIA at his ranch in Crawford, TX.

—During the election dispute the CIA actually set up an office in Crawford, TX to pass intelligence to Mr. Bush and his advisers.

—In December 2000, during the transition, Mr. Bush met with Mr. Clinton for a two-hour one-on-one discussion of the national security and foreign policy challenges. Mr. Clinton says he told Mr. Bush that the biggest threat he will face would be Al Qaeda and Bin Ladin. Mr. Clinton also says that he told Mr. Bush that one of his biggest regrets is not capturing or killing Bin Ladin. (Mr. Bush later claimed that Mr. Clinton never told him any of the above.)

—CIA Deputy Director for operations James Pavitt testified that in early 2001 himself and George Tenet briefed then president-elect George W. Bush and Vice president-elect Dick Cheney on terrorism and Al Qaeda and told them that Usama Bin Ladin was the greatest threat facing the USA.

—In January 2001 counterterrorism expert Richard Clarke submitted a strategy paper to then National Security Adviser Condaleezza Rice, warning that Al Qaeda members were present in the USA, and requested an urgent meeting of "principals" to discuss the Al Qaeda threat. No meeting was held until September 4, 2001, a week before 9/11.

—During 2001 George Tenet briefed Mr. Bush on a daily basis through what is knows as the President's Daily Brief (PDB) on matters regarding threats and other operational information pertaining to Bin Ladin and Al Qaeda. From January 20, 2001 to September 10, 2001 there were more than **40** briefings that related to Bin Ladin.

—According to The 9/11 Commission Report, Mr. Bush on several occasions asked his advisors during the spring and early summer of 2001 if any of the Al Qaeda threats pointed to the U.S. homeland. In response, the CIA drafted a PDB on August 6, 2001 entitled "Bin Ladin Determined To Strike in US". The two CIA analysts who drafted the PDB believed that it represented the view that the threat of Al Qaeda was both current and serious. But when Mr. Bush testified before the 9/11 Commission he claimed that the PDB was "historical" in nature and didn't give him any information that he could act on. He also said he did not discuss the August 6 PDB with either the Attorney General or his National Security Adviser. Here is what the PDB told Mr. Bush:

Bin Ladin Determined To Strike in US

Clandestine, foreign government, and media reports indicate Bin Ladin since 1997 has wanted to conduct terrorist attacks in the US. Bin Ladin implied in US television interviews in 1997 and 1998 that his followers would follow the example of World Trade Center bomber Ramzi Yousef and "bring the fighting to America."

After US missile strikes on his base in Afghanistan in 1998, Bin Laden told followers he wanted to retaliate in Washington, according to a [-] service.

An Egyptian Islamic Jihad (EIJ) operative told an [-] service at the same time that Bin Ladin was planning to exploit the operative's access to the US to mount a terrorist strike.

The millennium plotting in Canada in 1999 may have been part of Bin Ladin's first serious attempt to implement a terrorist strike in the US. Convicted plotter Ahmed Ressam has told the FBI that he conceived the idea to attack Los Angeles International Airport himself, but that Bin Ladin Lieutenant Abu Zubaydah encouraged him and helped facilitate the operation. Rassam also said that in 1998 Abu Zubaydah was planning his own US attack.

Ressam says Bin Ladin was aware of the Los Angeles operation.

Although Bin Ladin has not succeeded, his attacks against the US Embassies in Kenya and Tanzania in 1998 demonstrate that he prepares operations years in advance and is not deterred by setbacks. Bin Ladin associates surveilled our Embassies in Nairobi and Dar es Salaam as early as 1993, and some members of the Nairobi cell planning the bombings were arrested and deported in 1997.

Al-Qa'ida members—including some who are US citizens—have resided in or traveled to the US for years, and the group apparently maintains a support structure that could aid attacks. Two al-Qua'da members found guilty in the conspiracy to bomb our embassies in East Africa were US citizens, and a senior EIJ member lived in California in the mid-1990's.

A clandestine source said in 1998 that a Bin Ladin cell in New York was recruiting Muslim-American youth for attacks.

We have not been able to corroborate some of the more sensational threat reporting, such as that from a [-] service in 1998 saying that Bin Ladin wanted to hijack a US aircraft to gain the release of "Blind Shaykh" 'Umar' Abd al-Rahman and other US-held extremists.

Nevertheless, FBI information since that time indicates patterns of suspicious activity in the country consistent with preparations for hijackings or other types of attacks, including recent surveillance of federal buildings in New York.

The FBI is conducting approximately 70 full field investigations throughout the US that it considers Bin Ladin-related. CIA and the FBI are investigating a call to our Embassy in the UAE in May saying that a group of Bin Ladin supporters was in the US planning attacks with explosives.

—From August 6, 2001 to September 11, 2001 there were *no* further discussion or meeting between Mr. Bush and his top advisers regarding Al Qaeda and Bin Ladin.

Hence, if one wants to play the blame game the way O'Reilly does, one can make a case that pre 9/11 the Bush Administration did nothing to stop or disrupt Al Qaeda despite being told repeatedly of the danger. **But I'm not going to make that case, because I don't think it is fair to blame either President Bill Clinton or President George W. Bush for the Al Qaeda build-up leading to the 9/11 tragedy.** The fact is that pre 9/11, no one would have supported a ground war against the Taliban to destroy Al Qaeda the same way they supported the Afghan war post 9/11, and for anyone to claim otherwise is intellectually dishonest. The 9/11 Commission Report put it best when it said:

> "Officials in both the Clinton and Bush Administrations regarded a full U.S. invasion of Afghanistan as practically inconceivable before 9/11. It was never the subject of formal interagency deliberation."[2]

To further support my argument I quote no other than Donald Rumsfeld, who's not a dove by any measure, who said the following when he testified before the 9/11 Commission:

> "… But imagine that we were back before September 11th and that a U.S. president had looked at the information then available, gone before the Con-

gress and the world and said we need to invade Afghanistan and overthrow the Taliban and destroy the Al Qaeda terrorist network based on what little was known before September 11th. How many countries would have joined? Many? Any? Not likely. We would have heard objections to preemption similar to those voiced before the coalition launched Operation Iraqi Freedom. We would have been asked, how could you attack Afghanistan when it was Al Qaeda that attacked us, not the Taliban? How can you go to war when countries in the region don't support you? Won't launching such an invasion actually provoke terrorist attacks against the United States? I agree with those who have testified here today—Mrs. Albright, Secretary Cohen and others—that unfortunately history shows that it can take a tragedy like September 11th to waken the world to the need for action ..."

I agree with Mr. Rumsfeld one hundred percent. He is right. No one could have put it better than the way he did above. I'm not a fan of Mr. Rumsfeld, but I admire his frankness and his outspokenness. In this case he is fair and honest and he must be given credit for it. So it is within this context that we have to analyze pre 9/11 policy. Bill O'Reilly wants to apply a post 9/11 perspective to the Clinton Administration's foreign policy decisions. That is dishonest analysis, because it's analysis done with the benefit of hindsight after the fact. The Clinton Administration's policy towards Bin Ladin and Al Qaeda has to be analyzed in the paradigm within which it took place. The fact is that Pre 9/11, a fully-fledged ground war against the Taliban and Al Qaeda was simply not an option, and it is within that context that one has to examine the Clinton Administration's policy. And when you do, you will find that the Clinton Administration was hard at work on multiple fronts dealing with the threat. O'Reilly wants you to believe that Mr. Clinton and his staff were asleep, did not recognize the threat, and made no attempt to deal with the situation. That is a lie. Here are the facts:

Sudan

When the State Department learned in late 1995 that the Sudanese government was considering expelling Bin Ladin from Sudan, they pushed the U.S. Ambassador in Sudan to encourage the Sudanese government to go thru with the plan. The Saudi government however refused to allow Bin Laden to return to Saudi Arabia, citing the fact that they had already revoked his Saudi citizenship. Hence, Bin Ladin ended up moving to Afghanistan. Many right-wing Clinton haters, including Bill O'Reilly, had alleged, and some continue to allege onto this day, that the Sudanese government offered Bin Ladin to Mr. Clinton "on a silver platter". The 9/11 Commission investigated this charge and found no evidence that the Sudanese government ever offered to turn Bin Ladin over to the United States, or to any other country for that matter. The CIA officer who held the one-on-one meeting with the Sudanese Defense Minister at the time confirmed that no such offer was ever made. In any case, even if Sudan had offered to turn Bin Ladin over to the United States, the United States did not have any indictment pending against him at that time, and would have run into legal difficulties holding him indefinitely. There was no Patriot Act back then. (Eventually, a Grand Jury in New York did hand down a sealed indictment against Bin Ladin on June 10, 1998 on charges of "conspiracy to attack US defense installations".) The CIA was willing to work on a plan to apprehend Bin Ladin if another country was willing to imprison him, but as it turned out, the Sudanese government did not notify the United States of Bin Ladin's departure until two days after he had actually left. Bin Laden moved to Afghanistan.

Covert Action

In 1996 the CIA set up a special unit called "The Bin Ladin Unit", whose job it was to analyze intelligence on Bin Ladin and develop plans to go after him. In the fall of 1997 the Bin Ladin unit developed a rough plan to capture Bin Ladin. The plan involved using the Afghan tribals to capture Bin Ladin and handing him over to either the United States or an Arab country to stand trial. At first, the CIA contemplated an ambush style assault against Bin Ladin when he traveled between Kandahar and where he used to live. Kandahar was the Taliban Capital in Afghanistan at that time, and Bin Ladin was living in an area called Tarnak Farms, which was located in an isolated desert area on the outskirts of Kandahar airport. The CIA had learnt that at times he would travel from Tarnak Farms to Kandahar where he sometimes stayed at night. The plan however was dropped because the Afghan tribals claimed that they had tried such a plan before and it failed.

The next idea was to conduct a nighttime raid on Bin Ladin's residence at Tarnak Farms. Tarnak Farms was actually a compound bounded by a 10-foot wall and containing about 80 buildings made from concrete or mud. The CIA was able to completely map the entire site, and even identified the various houses that were inhabited by the wives of Bin Ladin. Even more impressive, the CIA was able to pinpoint what they believed to be the house that Bin Ladin himself was likely to sleep in. The plan to raid Tarnak farms involved using two groups of Afghan tribals. One group would first subdue the guards, stealthily enter the compound, seize Bin Ladin and take him to a desert site outside Kahdahar, where the second group was waiting. The second group was then supposed to take him to a second site that the CIA is familiar with, and one that the CIA had used before in a similar though smaller operation. There, a CIA plane was supposed to be on standby ready to fly Bin Ladin either to New York or an Arab Capital, or wherever he was to be arraigned for the charges against him.

By the fall of 1997 the CIA ran two complete rehearsals of the plan in the United States, and in May 1998 they ran a final graded rehearsal even bringing in some Afghan tribals to participate. The plan, however, was never implemented. Even though the officers in the Bin Ladin Unit believed that the plan was work-able and may succeed, the CIA Director George Tenet told the 9/11 Commis-sion that based on recommendations from his chief operations officers, he decide to "turn off" the operation, and hence the plan was *never* presented to President Clinton for a decision.

Nevertheless, Richard Clarke had kept pushing the Pentagon to consider some sort of military action against Bin Ladin and Al Qaeda. On June 2, 1998 the then Chairman of the Joint Chiefs of Staff General Hugh Shelton instructed general Zinni at Central Command to put together a plan. During the first week of July, General Zinni submitted a plan that proposed firing Tamahawk cruise missiles against eight terrorist camps in Afghanistan, including Bin Ladin's compound at Tarnak Farms.

As it happened, the next opportunity to strike at Bin Ladin came within the next two months. On the morning of August 7, 1998 a bomb exploded at the U.S. Embassy in Nairobi, Kenya, killing 12 U.S. citizens, 32 Foreign Service Nationals (FSNs), and 247 Kenyan citizens. Approximately 5,000 Kenyans, 6 U.S. citizens, and 13 FSNs were injured. Almost simultaneously, a bomb deto-nated outside the U.S. Embassy in Dar es Salaam, Tanzania, killing 7 FSNs and 3 Tanzanian citizens, and injuring 1U.S. citizen and 76 Tanzanians. Based on unusually good intelligence obtained by the CIA from their monitoring of an Al Qaeda cell in Nairobi, Kenya, the CIA almost immediately confirmed that Al Qaeda was behind the attacks. It was decided that the USA should respond with Tamahawk cruise missiles, since there were already plans on the table.

On the day after the embassy bombing, the CIA received information that ter-rorist leaders, including Bin Ladin, would be meeting at a camp near Khowst, Afghanistan, to plan future attacks. Sandy Berger, Richard Clarke, and George Tenet all agreed that the gathering should be attacked, and the Pentagon briefed President Clinton about the plan on August 12 and 14. It was also debated whether to strike other targets outside of Afghanistan. The intelligence services had two other targets on its list. One was a pharmaceutical plant called al Shifa in Khartoum, Sudan, which was believed to be producing EMPTA, a precursor chemical for VX, a nerve gas used exclusively for mass killings. The second was a tannery also in Sudan owned by Bin Ladin. The rational for bombing the tannery was that it would hurt Bin Ladin financially, while the argument for destroying al Shifa was obviously that it would decrease the possibility of Bin Ladin ever getting nerve gas to use in any later attack. On the morning of August 20, 1998 President Clinton signed off on bombing the terrorist camps in Khowst, Afghanistan, and the pharmaceutical plant in Khartoum, Sudan. He decided against striking the tannery on the reasoning that innocent people would be killed and Bin Ladin may not suffer significantly.

Later that day, August 20, 1998, the air strikes went ahead. Tamahawk cruise missiles were fired from Navy vessels in the Arabian Sea. Although most of them hit their intended targets, neither Bin Ladin nor any other terrorist leader was killed. George Tenet concluded, based on after-action review, that the strikes had killed 20-30 people who were in the camps, but probably missed Bin Ladin by a few hours. (Cruise missiles take time to get to their targeted location because they are fired from far away, so if the individual being targeted moves from that location while the missile is en route to that location he will escape unharmed). Speculation was that Pakistani officials tipped off either the Taliban or Bin Ladin. The problem was that the United States had to notify Pakistan of the strikes for two reasons: Firstly, the cruise missiles had to cross Pakistani's airspace in order to travel to Afghanistan. Secondly, if Pakistan wasn't notified they might think they were being attacked by India and might respond accordingly.

The missile strikes also drew intense criticism from the media, the American public, and the Congress of the United States (particularly Republicans). The Sudanese government denied that al Shifa produced nerve gas and they invited journalist to visit what was left of the site. The problem was further compounded by the fact that President Clinton at that time was embroiled in the Monica Lewinsky scandal, and his critics invoked the "Wag the Dog" theory. (In 1997 a movie by the name of "Wag the Dog" came out featuring a president who faked a war overseas in order to divert attention from a domestic scandal at home.) Mr. Clinton's critics argued that life was imitating art, and Mr. Clinton created a foreign policy crisis in order to shift focus away from his personal problems.

Anti-Terrorism Legislation

In February 1995, President Clinton submitted proposals to Congress to extend federal criminal jurisdiction to make it easier to deport terrorists, and to act against terrorist fund-raising. After the Oklahoma City bombing in April, President Clinton proposed further amendments to Congress to increase wiretap and electronic surveillance authority for the FBI, to require that explosives carry trace-able taggants, and to provide substantial new money for the FBI, the CIA, and local police. In June he issued a classified directive, Presidential Decision Direc-tive 39, which said that the United States should "deter, defeat and respond vig-orously to all terror attacks on our territory and against our citizens".

During 1995 and 1996 President Clinton devoted considerable time to seek-ing cooperation from other nations in denying sanctuary to terrorists. He pro-posed significantly larger budgets for the FBI, with much of the increase designated for counter-terrorism. For the CIA, he essentially stopped cutting allocations and supported requests for supplemental funds for counter-terrorism. When he was reelected in 1996, President Clinton mentioned terrorism first in a list of several challenges facing the United States. Later, he issued Presidential Decision Directive number 63, which defined the elements of the United States infrastructure and considered ways to protect.

Funding for Counter-terrorism

According to Daniel Benjamin and Steven Simon in their Book *The Age of Sacred Terror*, spending on counter-terrorism by the Clinton Administration nearly doubled from 1996 (after the Khobar Towers bombing) to the end of President Clinton's second term. Mr. Benjamin and Mr. Simon should know, because they were former Director for counter-terrorism and former Senior Director for counter-terrorism respectively at the NSA. In 1996 the figure was $5.7 billion, but by 2001 it had swelled to $11.3 Billion. $400 million was spent in 1996 on upgrading the aviation security system, which produced new high-tech baggage screening devices, "trace detectors" for finding minute residue of explosives, and 140 more Customs Inspectors. An additional $700 million was spent recruiting and training five hundred new FBI counter-terrorism agents. The result was that by the end of Mr. Clinton's presidency counter-terrorism agents had doubled.[3]

Working with Pakistan

President Clinton tried hard to get the Pakistani government to use their political influence and pressure the Taliban to stop sheltering Bin Ladin, and expel him from Afghanistan. He also tried to get the Pakistanis to use their economic lever-age to inflict pain on the Taliban Regime, since the Pakistanis controlled fuel shipments to Afghanistan, and also controlled much of Afghanistan's trade that flowed through Karachi.

However, as we shall see later, dealing with Pakistan is and always has been a complex issue for any American President. The masses in Pakistan are anti-American, so even though the leader of Pakistan may be a Moderate who is willing to work with America on serious issues, that leader can only go so far or else face internal unrest and unpopularity.

In 1998 President Clinton invited Pakistan's Prime Minister Nawaz Sharif to Washington, where they talked mostly about India, but also discussed Bin Ladin. However, Mr. Clinton did not obtain any commitment from the Pakistani leader. After Sharif returned back to Pakistan Mr. Clinton called him and raised the issue of Bin Ladin again. This time Sharif promised to talk to the Taliban. In June 1999 President Clinton again contacted Mr. Sharif partly to discuss the crisis with India but also to urge Sharif in the strongest possible terms to persuade the Taliban to expel Bin Ladin. Mr. Clinton floated the idea to Mr. Sharif that Pakistan use its control over oil supplies to the Taliban and over Afghan imports through Karachi to pressure the Taliban. Mr. Sharif suggested instead that Pakistani forces might try to capture Bin Ladin themselves. President Clinton was skeptical but nevertheless gave the idea his blessing. President Clinton again met with Mr. Sharif in Washington in early July 1999 mainly to seal the Pakistani Prime Minister's decision to withdraw from the Kargil confrontation in Kashmir, but Mr. Clinton used the occasion to complain about Pakistan's failure to take effective action with respect to the Taliban and Bin Ladin. Mr. Sharif fell back to his earlier proposal that Pakistani forces try to capture Bin Ladin, and won approval for U.S. assistance to train Pakistani Special Forces for an operation against Bin Ladin. However, this all came tumbling down in October 1999 when Mr. Sharif tried to fire his army chief of staff, General Pervez Musharraf. Musharraf's plane was returning from Sri Lanka, and Mr. Sharif ordered that Musharraf's plane be not allowed to land in Pakistan, in effect exiling Musharraf. But the army rebelled, deposed Sharif, and jailed him. Musharraf became the new Pakistani leader.

The tensions between Mr. Sharif and General Musharraf had been extremely high. Mr. Sharif had been caught between a rock and a hard place. On the one hand Mr. Clinton was pressuring him to withdraw from Kargil, while on the other hand General Musharraf and the Pakistani military were accusing him of "selling out". In the end, American pressure did work to get Pakistan to back off from Kargil and avoid a nuclear confrontation with India, but the negotiations resulted in terrorism itself being put on the back burner, since at that moment the focus was more on avoiding a nuclear confrontation between India and Pakistan than on pressuring the Pakistanis to squeeze the Taliban.

In April 2000 President Clinton made a trip to India, the first presidential visit to that country by a U.S. president in almost twenty years. Mr. Clinton insisted on making a stop over in Islamabad, Pakistan, but everyone advised him against doing so for security reasons, since anti-American Jihadists operated with virtual impunity in Pakistan. The Secret Service felt that it could not fulfill its mission of protecting the President. There was danger to Air Force One from ground fire, and no one trusted the Pakistani military to keep travel routes in the country secret or secure. In a meeting with Mr. Clinton, the head of the presidential detail, Larry Cockell, told Mr. Clinton directly that the Secret Service would not be able to protect him. Mr. Clinton, however, overrode their concerns and insisted on making the stop over in Pakistan. (Incidentally, this was not the first time Mr. Clinton overrode the advice of the Secret Service in making a foreign trip. Mr. Clinton had similarly overridden the Secret Service's recommendation in 1999 for a trip to Kosovo when the Secret Service was fearful that Serb forces might attack Air Force One from the ground. Mr. Clinton went ahead with that trip.) In the end, he slipped away from India to Islamabad in a small G-5 jet belonging to the CIA, while Air Force One flew in as a decoy. He became the first U.S. President to visit Pakistan in many years. It was both a personal risk as well as a political risk. But he reportedly felt that he had to go because he believed that the U.S. must remain involved with both the issue of the India-Pakistan confrontation as well as the issue of Bin Ladin, the Taliban, and terrorism. He met twice with President Musharraf, and though the subject of terrorism was kept brief, Mr. Clinton pressed Mr. Musharraf very hard to have him use Pakistan's influence with the Taliban to get Bin Ladin. Mr. Musharraf promised that "he will do all he can", but given the tenuous position of Mr. Musharraf himself, one can understand why he couldn't push too hard. But again, Mr. Clinton must be given due credit for taking the bold steps he did.

Terrorist Funding

After the embassy bombings in East Africa in 1998, an interagency committee on terrorist funding was created. It recommended that President Clinton designate Bin Ladin and Al Qaeda as subject to sanctions under the International Emergency Powers Act. Mr. Clinton followed their recommendation, and this enabled the Treasury Department's Office of Foreign Assets Control (OFAC) to search for and seize any Bin Ladin or Al Qaeda assets that reached the U.S. financial system. President Clinton extended the sanctions to cover the Taliban in July 1999 for their harboring of Bin Ladin. This resulted in OFAC blocking more than $34 million in Taliban assets held in U.S. banks. A further $215 million in gold and $2 million in demand deposits that belonged to the Afghan Central Bank, and held at Federal Reserve Bank of New York, were frozen.

Sanctions against the Taliban

In October 1999 the United States convinced the United Nations to *unanimously* adopt sanctions against the Taliban. Resolution 1267 imposed wide-ranging sanctions against the regime except for food and humanitarian assistance. The Clinton Administration also took action against the Afghan National Airline, Ariana. It was suspected that Ariana transported terrorists, their funds, and their materials around the world for planning and conducting terrorist activities. The Clinton Administration imposed sanctions against Ariana and convinced many countries around the world to ban Ariana from landing at their airports. One of the major effects of the sanction was that it froze money Ariana kept in a Citibank account in India. The action against Ariana did hurt the Taliban because not only was Ariana a major source of income but it was also an important link to the outside world.

Raising National awareness

Throughout his presidency, President Clinton did not fail to communicate the seriousness of the threat posed by terrorism to America (and to the world). However, the media and other sections of American society did not share the same sense of urgency as Mr. Clinton. He tried but did not gain the traction necessary to spurn serious discussion and debate in the media and other public venues regarding how the United States should deal with the growing threat of terrorism, and Al Qaeda in particular. The media never bothered to analyze and discuss his warnings, and in fact, many felt that he was over-stating the issue. Nevertheless, his tenure as President was filled with speeches and comments attempting to bring the issue of terrorism to the front and center.

Immediately after taking office, President Clinton decided to coordinate counter-terrorism from the White House. In his State of the Union speech in January 1995 he promised "comprehensive legislation to strengthen our hand in combating terrorists, whether they strike at home or abroad". In May 1998 in a speech to the Naval Academy, President Clinton continued his efforts to raise the level of awareness in the United States and around the world when he said the following:

> "First we will use our new integrated approach to intensify the fight against all forms of terrorism; to capture terrorists, no matter where they hide; to work with other nations to eliminate terrorist sanctuaries overseas; to respond rapidly and effectively to protect Americans from terrorism at home and abroad. Second, we will launch a comprehensive plan to detect, deter, and defend

against attacks on our critical infrastructures, our power systems, water supplies, police, fire, and medical services, air traffic control, financial services,
telephone systems and computer networks ... Third, we will undertake a con-
certed effort to protect our people in the event these terrible weapons are ever
unleashed by a rogue state, a terrorist group, or an international criminal organization.... Finally, we must do more to protect our civilian population from
biological weapons."

In his final State of the Union Speech Mr. Clinton warned:

"I predict to you, when most of us are long gone, but sometime in the next ten
to twenty years, the major security threat this country will face will come from
the enemies of the nation-state: the narcotraffickers and the terrorists and the
organized criminals, who will be organized together, working together, with
increasing access to even more sophisticated chemical and biological weapons."

Executive Order 12333

Issued on December 4, 1981 by President Reagan, Executive Order 12333 forbid
the United States from engaging in assassination. Here is the exact text of the relevant sections of Executive Order 12333 as it pertains to assassinations:

2.11 *Prohibition on Assassination.* No person employed by or acting on behalf of
the United States Government shall engage in, or conspire to engage in, assassination.
2.12 *Indirect Participation.* No agency of the Intelligence Community shall participate in or request any person to undertake activities forbidden by this Order.

President Clinton was bound by this Executive Order. Had he ordered the
assassination of Bin Ladin, he would have been directly in breach of U.S. Law,
and he probably would have been held accountable for his actions. Of course, it
was just an Executive Order, and President Clinton could have tried to change it
if he felt that it was absolutely necessary to do so. But who would have supported
him changing it at that time? It would have been seen as an extraordinary move
and his critics would have objected. President Clinton did, however, try to skirt
around the Order, and he should be given credit for it. On December 21, 1998,
Mr. Clinton's National Security team decided to strengthen an earlier document
that authorized only the capture of Bin Ladin, not killing him. Sandy Berger presented the revised document to Mr. Clinton on Christmas Eve of 1998, and Mr.

Clinton signed off on it. The new document allowed the killing of Bin Ladin if the CIA and the Afghan tribals came to the judgment that capturing him wasn't feasible. The rationale used to justify the new document was a scenario where the tribals try to capture Bin Ladin, a shootout ensues, and Bin Ladin is killed. The Clinton Administration's position therefore would have been that, under the law of armed conflict, killing a person who posed an imminent threat to the United States would be an act of self-defense, not an assassination. So Mr. Clinton was prepared to take extraordinary measures against Bin Ladin, but had to navigate carefully through the loops of U.S. law. Those who accuse him of timidity and temerity have no basis for their argument.

Footnotes to Chapter Eight

1) Who's Looking Out for You, Bill O'Reilly, page 61.

2) The 9/11 Commission Report, page 349.

3) The Age Of Sacred Terror, Daniel Benjamin and Steven Simon, page 348.

978-0-595-43408-4
0-595-43408-8

Printed in the United States
76628LV00004B/184